National Police Library
NPIA
Bramshill
Hook, Hampshire
RG27 0JW

Return to an Address of the Honorable the House of Commons
dated 12 March 2009
for the

The Protection of Children in England: A Progress Report

The Lord Laming

Ordered by the House of Commons to be printed on
12 March 2009

D1344850

HC 330   LONDON: THE STATIONERY OFFICE   £19.15

CONTENTS

The front cover picture was drawn by Caitlin, aged 8 years.
The back cover picture was drawn by Megan, aged 12 years.

INTRODUCTION

> "Children become the victims or the beneficiaries of adult actions."
>
> Hugh Cunningham[1]

'Please keep me safe'. This simple but profoundly important hope is the very minimum upon which every child and young person should be able to depend. Sadly, sometimes even our imaginations fail to help us understand the dependency of young children or the vulnerability of adolescents, regardless of their displays of bravado. Most adults recognise that children and young people need security, stability, love and encouragement. As the Chief Rabbi Sir Jonathan Sacks put it, "Children grow to fill the space we create for them, and if it's big, they grow tall".[2] The years of childhood pass all too quickly and become the foundation upon which the rest of life depends.

Policies, legislation, structures and procedures are, of course, of immense importance, but they serve only as the means of securing better life opportunities for each young person. It is the robust and consistent implementation of these policies and procedures which keeps children and young people safe. For example, organisational boundaries and concerns about sharing information must never be allowed to put in jeopardy the safety of a child or young person. Whilst children and young people's safety is a matter for us all, a heavy responsibility has rightly been placed on the key statutory services to ensure it happens.

But it serves no one, least of all children, if the scale of the task is under estimated. For example, Department for Children, Schools and Families (DCSF) information shows that on 31 March 2008, 37,000 children[3] were the subjects of care orders (of 60,000 children looked

1   Cunningham, Hugh, *The Invention of Childhood* (BBC Books, 2006)
2   The Chief Rabbi, Sir Jonathan Sacks, on 'Thought for the Day', BBC Radio 4, 12 December 2008. Quoted with the permission of The Chief Rabbi
3   DCSF SSDA903 data collection 31 March 2008 (available online at www.dcsf.gov.uk/rsgateway/DB/SFR/s000810/index.shtml)

after by local authorities[4]) and 29,000 children[5] were the subject of child protection plans. Home Office data shows that in 2007/08, 55 children[6] were killed by their parents or by someone known to the child.

It would be unreasonable to expect that the sudden and unpredictable outburst by an adult towards a child can be prevented. But that is entirely different from the failure to protect a child or young person already identified as being in danger of deliberate harm. The death of a child in these circumstances is a reproach to us all.

Following the case of 'Baby P', the Secretary of State for Children, Schools and Families, the Rt Hon Ed Balls MP, acted decisively. On 17 November 2008 he commissioned me to provide an urgent report on the progress being made across the country to implement effective arrangements for safeguarding children. His letter is reproduced at Appendix 1. The kernel of the task was to evaluate the good practice that has been developed since the publication of the report of the Independent Statutory Inquiry following the death of Victoria Climbié, to identify the barriers that are now preventing good practice becoming standard practice, and recommend actions to be taken to make systematic improvements in safeguarding children across the country.

The Government deserves credit for the legislation and guidance that has been put in place to safeguard children and promote the welfare of children over the last five years. *Every Child Matters*[7] clearly has the support of professionals, across all of the services, who work with children and young people. The interagency guidance *Working Together to Safeguard Children*[8] provides a sound framework for professionals to protect children and promote their welfare. New models for early intervention developed nationally and delivered locally through extended schools and Sure Start Children's Centres have established a solid foundation on which to build more imaginative and flexible responses to the needs of children and

4 DCSF CPR3 data collection 31 March 2008
   (available online at www.dcsf.gov.uk/rsgateway/DB/SFR/s000811/index.shtml)
5 DCSF CPR3 data collection 31 March 2008
   (available online at www.dcsf.gov.uk/rsgateway/DB/SFR/s000811/index.shtml)
6 Homicides, Firearm Offences and Intimate Violence 2007/08 (Supplementary Volume 2 to Crime in England and Wales 2007/08), David Povey (ed.), Kathryn Coleman, Peter Kaiza and Stephen Roe (Home Office, available online at www.homeoffice.gov.uk/rds/pdfs09/hosb0209.pdf) Additional offences where suspect is unknown not recorded here
7 HM Government, *Every Child Matters: Change for Children* (2004)
8 HM Government, *Working Together to Safeguard Children: A guide to inter-agency working to safeguard and promote the welfare of children* (2006)

families. However, whilst the improvements in the services for children and families, in general, are welcome it is clear that the need to protect children and young people from significant harm and neglect is ever more challenging. There now needs to be a step change in the arrangements to protect children from harm. It is essential that action is now taken so that as far as humanly possible children at risk of harm are properly protected.

One of the main challenges is to ensure that leaders of local services effectively to translate policy, legislation and guidance into day-to-day practice on the frontline of every service. As the Society of Local Authority Chief Executives and Senior Managers (SOLACE) advised me in their evidence to this report:

"Chief Executives are the best paid most senior members of staff in councils. Notwithstanding the statutory role of other staff, now including Directors of Children's Services, Chief Executives should accept their role in setting and securing high standards and hiring and where necessary firing expert staff."

The personal accountability of the most senior managers in all of the public services now needs to be fully understood.

Leaders of local services must recognise the importance of early intervention and ensure that their departments support children as soon as they are recognised as being 'in need', averting escalation to the point at which families are in crisis.

Frontline staff in each of the key services have a demanding task. Their work requires not only knowledge and skill but also determination, courage, and an ability to cope with sometimes intense conflict. This must be recognised in their training, case-loads, supervision and conditions of service, and their managers must recognise that anxiety undermines good practice. Staff supervision and the assurance of good practice must become elementary requirements in each service. More should be done to ensure the well-being and confidence of the staff who undertake such an important task on behalf of us all.

To support staff in this vitally important task of protecting children, central government and local agencies must immediately take the following action:

First and foremost, the Secretaries of State for Health, Justice, the Home Office and Children, Schools and Families must collaborate in the setting of explicit strategic priorities for the protection of children and young people for each of the key frontline services and ensure sufficient resources are in place to deliver these priorities. There is little hope for the full integration and joined-up working of local and regional services if the same approach is not fully realised in central government. Now is the time to address this imbalance.

Secondly, the Government must immediately inject greater energy and drive into the implementation of change and support local improvement by establishing a powerful National Safeguarding Delivery Unit to report directly to Cabinet through the Families, Children and Young People Sub-Committee, and to report annually to Parliament. This multi-disciplinary unit must be led by someone with great authority, specialist knowledge and obvious ambition for improving outcomes for children and young people and for the quality of services they receive, especially for children in danger of deliberate abuse or neglect. This flexible and agile team must be able to draw on staff with direct frontline experience from across police, health and children's services along with staff from central government who can act quickly to offer their expertise to improve outcomes for children. The unit would not have to be a permanent presence, but it is needed for a short time to bring coherence, drive and energy to the implementation of change through government departments and local services whose work is to protect children. Initially, the unit's main task will be to drive the implementation of the recommendations of this report, working with the Cabinet Sub-Committee on Families, Children and Young People to set and publish challenging timescales for each recommendation. More detail on the unit is given in Chapter 6.

Thirdly, the Secretary of State for Children, Schools and Families must immediately address the inadequacy of the training and supply of frontline social workers. The message of this report is clear: without the necessary specialist knowledge and skills social workers must not be allowed to practise in child protection. A high priority must be given to establishing a new postgraduate programme to be completed by all children's social workers as soon as is practicable. A programme of management training should be put in place and steps taken to ensure there is strong and determined leadership in every local authority. No time should be lost in demanding best practice for some of the most vulnerable children in our society. Issues of low morale and esteem within the service must be rectified. In this context, I welcome the decision by ministers to establish the Social Care Task

Force led by Moira Gibb, the well-respected Chief Executive of the London Borough of Camden.

Fourthly, the Secretary of State for Health must immediately address the wariness of staff throughout the health services to engage with child protection work. GPs, community nurses and paediatricians must be helped to develop a wider range of skills and become very much more confident in this important area of their work. Of greater challenge still is the need to address the status, training and responsibilities carried by health visitors. Evidence to this progress report makes clear that there are a number of challenges to be addressed in this service. The work of health visitors requires immediate action to increase the numbers, confidence and competence of staff.

Fifthly, the Home Secretary must urgently address the adequacy of the resources devoted to police child protection teams, the specialist training of these staff, the vacancy rates, the status of this work and the quality of service provided.

Sixthly, the Secretary of State for Justice should take immediate action to shorten the time taken in court processes relating to the care of children. In 2008/09 the average time taken for a case to come to court was 45 weeks,[9] an unacceptably long time to leave a child in limbo at this formative stage in his or her life. When the state is seeking to make a care order, there should be no budgetary impediment to this. The increase in court fees for care order applications by local authorities was unhelpful, and was made worse by the transfer of the money into the general funding of local government. The Ministry of Justice should make arrangements for these fees to be reconsidered.

The remainder of this document, and its recommendations, are aimed at making sure that good practice becomes standard practice in every service. This includes recommendations on improving the inspection of safeguarding services and the quality of Serious Case Reviews as well as recommendations on improving the help and support children receive when they are at risk of harm. The utility of the policy and

---

9   Family Court, County and High Courts 2008/09 provisional data, Ministry of Justice, England and Wales. Notes:
   (1)   Family Court data is from Family Case Tracker and FamilyMan. County Court and High Court data is from FamilyMan
   (2)   Figures are for April to September 2008
   (3)   Care and supervision orders are included and are counted by child for Family Court figures and by order for County Court and High Court

legislation has been pressed on me by contributors throughout this report. In such circumstances it is hard to resist the urge to respond by saying to each of the key services, if that is so "NOW JUST DO IT!"

With greater ambition and determination I am sure it can be done. Now is the time to prove that the well-being of every child and young person really does matter, not least because the UN Convention on the Rights of the Child (Article 6) states, "Parties recognise that every child has the right to life. Parties shall ensure to the maximum extent possible the survival and development of the child".[10] It has been put to me that it is inevitable that some adults, for whatever reason, will deliberately harm children. That may well be so. Nevertheless, it cannot be beyond our wit to put in place ways of identifying early those children at risk of deliberate harm, and to put in place the means of securing their safety and proper development.

In general, families are best placed to care for children and promote their welfare. Fortunately the vast majority of parents seek the best for their children and, entirely rightly, the state supports them in this important task. However, parenthood incorporates not only rights but also responsibilities: it is a lifetime commitment. Particular mention should be made of the part to be played by fathers, not least as good role models.

Because this report has been conducted against a tight timescale I wish to record my thanks to the many organisations that responded so quickly and all of those that have become involved in other ways. In the course of the report I received over 100 written submissions from key stakeholders and over 200 letters from a range of individuals including professionals across the children's workforce. The report team visited six local areas and met with key staff from local authorities, education, health and the police. The team hosted a series of seminars to gather the views of national stakeholders, local leaders and frontline staff. I and other members in the team met national stakeholders, trade unions, officials of government departments, and some Members of Parliament. I am also most grateful to 11 Million and to Dr Roger Morgan for consulting young people and passing on to me their views and experiences of services for children and young people. It is the evidence, information and opinions gathered from all of these sources that underpin this report.

10 Available online at www.unhchr.ch/html/menu3/b/k2crc.htm

I could not have undertaken this report without the strong support of a team of skilled, enthusiastic and very committed colleagues. Their names are recorded in Appendix 3. A glossary of abbreviations used throughout the report is at Appendix 2.

The Lord Laming

March 2009

PROGRESS

"Be gentle with the young."

Juvenal[11]

1.1   Children are our future. We depend on them growing up to become fulfilled citizens well able to contribute successfully to family life and to the wider society. It is of fundamental importance that the life and future development of each child is given equal importance. Every child needs to be nurtured and protected from harm. A great deal of progress has been made towards achieving this and the Government deserves credit for its policy of *Every Child Matters*. Yet recent events have shown that very much more needs to be done to ensure that the services are as effective as possible at working together to achieve positive outcomes for children.

Progress so far

1.2   This country has a long history of commitment to the protection of children and supporting their welfare. Many of those who contributed to this report have vast personal experience in grappling with these matters and there have been significant milestones along the way. At the level of frontline delivery, there is an impressive degree of individual commitment and enthusiasm for *Every Child Matters* and for the vision of what a 'good' childhood should be. Throughout children's services, police and health, there are many individuals who are making it their life's work to protect children and improve their well-being despite the fact that often this is a challenging task that can entail facing real conflict.

1.3   The last five years have been a particularly intense time of change. *Every Child Matters* came about as a direct result of a failure of the services to safeguard children with the death of Victoria Climbié and it still has overwhelming support across children's services and beyond. Central government and local agencies are now at the halfway point in this ten-year programme of change. The first five years have seen sound progress in legislative and structural terms. The introduction of a Cabinet Sub-Committee on Families, Children and Young People chaired by the Secretary of State for Children, Schools and Families and supported by a cross-government delivery board for the Public Service Agreement to improve children and young people's safety[12] are important and welcome developments. The Child Safety Reference Group utilises the experience of over 20 stakeholders to influence the safeguarding agenda. At local level, a great deal has been done to create new universal services for the under 5s, and ensure that support is in place for children and young people through early intervention and greater joint working through schools.

1.4   However, despite this encouraging start, there are real challenges still to address in safeguarding and child protection if children are to have services they can rely on when their own lives are in crisis.

The challenges that remain

1.5   *Working Together to Safeguard Children*[13] sets out sound practices for children's social workers and for other professionals which, if well understood and used intelligently and effectively will give children and young people better quality lives and, on occasion, save lives. However, the evidence is mixed on how well understood these processes are, and too often the findings of Serious Case Reviews demonstrate that simple steps from this guidance could have saved lives.[14] There are training and workforce issues to be resolved, and data systems that need to be improved to support professionals better, but ultimately the safety of a child depends on staff having the time, knowledge and skill to understand the child or young person and their family circumstances.

1.6   Despite considerable progress in interagency working, often driven by Local Safeguarding Children Boards and multi-agency teams who strive to help children and young people, there remain significant problems in the day-to-day reality of working across organisational boundaries and cultures, sharing information to protect children and a lack of feedback when professionals raise concerns about a child. Joint working between children's social workers, youth workers,

12 PSA Delivery Agreement 13: Improve children and young people's safety (HM Government, April 2008)
13 HM Government, *Working Together to Safeguard Children: A guide to interagency working to safeguard and promote the welfare of children* (2006)
14 Ofsted, *Learning lessons, taking action: Ofsted's evaluations of serious case reviews 1 April 2007 to 31 March 2008* (December 2008)

schools, early years, police and health too often depends on the commitment of individual staff and sometimes this happens despite, rather than because of, the organisational arrangements. This must be addressed by senior management in every service.

1.7 Undermining many attempts to protect children and young people and improve their well-being effectively is the low quality of training and support given to often over-stretched frontline staff across social care, health and police. Social work case-loads are often very high and more than 60 per cent of health visitor case-loads are above recommended levels.[15] The pressure of high case-loads is exacerbated by the fact that many social workers believe their training fails to prepare them for working with families in crisis. Within police forces the profile of child protection is variable with some forces (but by no means all) having reduced resources for child protection continually over the last three years and many contributors expressing concerns that vacancy rates are too high. There is a lack of high-quality specialist training on child protection across these services that undermines the good intentions of staff to do the best they can for the children they work with.

1.8 The issues outlined above have not had the priority they deserve over the last five years. In part, this may be due to the lack of effective challenge and support for improvement of safeguarding and child protection services across agencies. The inspection process has not been as effective in scrutinising practice in safeguarding as it has been in education, and the changes to the inspection framework announced recently are very much needed. The development function that the Commission for Social Care Inspection provided for children's social care has been lost and not effectively replaced or expanded to support safeguarding and child protection services across agencies (see Chapter 6).

Understanding the scale and complexity of need

1.9 Childhood and family life today is a complex matter and it is small wonder that there are still persistent misconceptions about child abuse and neglect. Safeguarding is not only about very young children or indeed issues of class, but it extends across society and through the

15 Unite/Community Practitioners' and Health Visitors' Association Omnibus Survey, 2008

teenage years. In 2007/08, 55 children were killed by someone known to the child (see graph below).[16]

Fig 1: Child homicides where the suspect was known to the victim

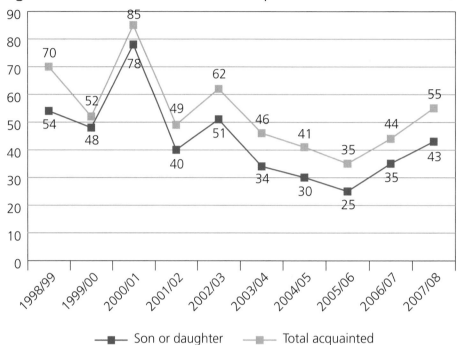

——■—— Son or daughter   ——■—— Total acquainted

Source: Police Crime Statistics, England and Wales.
Notes:
(1) As at November 2008; figures are subject to revision as cases are dealt with by the police and by the courts or as further information becomes available
(2) Child homicides including baby battering, neglect, excessive punishment
(3) Offences are shown according to the year in which the incident took place or the year in which any court decision was made
(4) If a child is killed by their adoptive parents they would be included in the son or daughter category but if the child is killed by their foster parents they would be included in the total acquainted category
(5) There are additional homicides where the suspect is unknown

1.10 Of the 11 million children in England[17] a total of 60,000 children were looked after by a local authority:[18] 37,000 were the subject of a care order (either full or interim)[19] and 29,000 were the subject of a Child Protection Plan.[20] In 2005, the last time national data was collected, a

16 Homicides, Firearm Offences and Intimate Violence 2007/08 (Supplementary Volume 2 to Crime in England and Wales 2007/08), David Povey (ed.), Kathryn Coleman, Peter Kaiza and Stephen Roe (Home Office, available online at www.homeoffice.gov.uk/rds/pdfs09/hosb0209.pdf) Additional offences where suspect is unknown not recorded here
17 Office for National Statistics (ONS) population estimates mid 2007, children aged under 18 years
18 Children in Need Census, February 2005
19 DCSF SSDA903 data collection, 31 March 2008 (available online at www.dcsf.gov.uk/rsgateway/DB/SFR/s000810/index.shtml)
20 DCSF CPR3 data collection, 31 March 2008 (available online at www.dcsf.gov.uk/rsgateway/DB/SFR/s000811/index.shtml)

total of 235,000 children[21] were described as being 'in need' and therefore requiring Section 17 support from the local authority.

---

11 million children in England. Of these …[22]

- 200,000 children live in households where there is a known high risk case of domestic abuse and violence[23]

- 235,000 are 'children in need' and in receipt of support from a local authority

- 60,000 are looked after by a local authority

- 37,000 are the subject of a care order

- 29,000 are the subject of a Child Protection Plan

- 1,300 are privately fostered[24]

- 300 are in secure children's homes[25]

1.11 The scale of need amongst children and young people, and the social, emotional and financial consequences of not improving their well-being and keeping them safe at an early stage in their lives, dictate that resolving the challenges laid out above should be one of the highest priorities for central and local government and the other key services. To effect a step change in services and to transform outcomes for children and young people the priority given to safeguarding must be achieved through strong and effective leadership, early intervention, adequate resources, and quality performance management, inspection and support.

21 Children in Need Census, February 2005

22 There is overlap between these categories: for example, a child who is living in a household with domestic violence may also be subject to a child protection plan

23 Co-ordinated Action Against Domestic Abuse based on their work to date on Multi-Agency Risk Assessment Conferences

24 DCSF private fostering return, 31 March 2008 (available on line at www.dcsf.gov.uk/rsgateway/DB/SFR/s000803/index.shtml)

25 DCSF SA1 Survey, England, 31 March 2008 (available on line at www.dcsf.gov.uk/rsgateway/DB/SFR/s000802/index.shtml)

LEADERSHIP AND ACCOUNTABILITY

"Children are our most valuable natural resource."

Herbert Hoover[26]

National leadership

2.1 Effective leadership sets the direction of an organisation, its culture and value system, and ultimately drives the quality and effectiveness of the services provided. It is essential that there is a sustained commitment to child protection and promoting the welfare of children at every level of government and in every one of the local services. The Cabinet Sub-Committee on Families, Children and Young People, chaired by the Secretary of State for Children, Schools and Families, carries ultimate responsibility for shaping a national safeguarding system that protects the safety and promotes welfare of children and young people in England. Building on progress already made, the Sub-Committee will need to continue to work to increase the momentum on delivering quality services at a local level and to raise the profile of children as a distinct group at all levels of government. The National Safeguarding Delivery Unit, which is explained further in Chapter 6 of this report, has a major contribution to make in this task.

2.2 Children are not 'little adults' and need particular support both as children, and for the particular condition or situation they find themselves in at any given moment in time. Within central government, the Department of Health, Ministry of Justice and Home Office, as departments with key safeguarding responsibilities, must recognise children as individuals with their own needs and ensure that their delivery strategies and services are appropriate and well quipped for the task.

26 Herbert Hoover (1874–1964), US President

Recommendations

The Home Secretary and the Secretaries of State for Children, Schools and Families, Health, and Justice must collaborate in the setting of explicit strategic priorities for the protection of children and young people and reflect these in the priorities of frontline services.

The Cabinet Sub-Committee on Families, Children and Young People should ensure that all government departments that impact on the safety of children take action to create a comprehensive approach to children through national strategies, the organisation of their central services, and the models they promote for the delivery of local services. This work should focus initially on changes to improve the child-focus of services delivered by the Department of Health, Ministry of Justice and Home Office.

Managing performance

2.3   Central government departments, particularly the Department for Children, Schools and Families (DCSF), the Department of Health, the Home Office, and the Ministry of Justice, need to collaborate to create an effective system of performance management that drives improvement in the quality of services designed to safeguard and promote the welfare of children and enable them to ensure they are meeting their responsibilities for keeping children safe. There is an urgent need to develop effective indicators for safeguarding children and young people that will drive positive improvements and secure better outcomes for them. The performance indicators currently in use for the safeguarding of children are inadequate for this task. Discussion with local authorities suggested that this was because of concerns that current indicators focus on processes and timescales, are not helpful in creating shared safeguarding priorities amongst statutory partners, are unclear in their impact upon positive outcomes for children and young people, and do not drive improved services. As a result, the take-up of these National Indicators (NIs) by local areas as part of their Local Area Agreements (LAAs) is low, with less than 10 per cent of local authorities choosing to adopt targets on most child protection indicators. A relatively small number of local authorities have opted to use the indicators as local targets.

2.4   It is undoubtedly not easy to find good measures of outcomes for safeguarding and child protection. However, it is important to continue to find ways of understanding the impact of work to keep children safe from harm. The Government's statutory DCSF targets should be reviewed to include safeguarding and child protection targets. The NI set also requires revision to ensure that the indicators available for inclusion in a LAA better describe improved outcomes and services for children and young people. These indicators must be specifically agreed by the Department of Health and the Home Office to ensure they are reflected in the performance management frameworks of Strategic Health Authorities (SHAs), Primary Care Trusts (PCTs) and Police Authorities. The complexity of managing performance across partner services should not be allowed to be a barrier to improving the safety of children and young people in England.

2.5   Central government departments need to communicate with increased clarity to local services their expectations around safeguarding and child protection. In particular, the Department of Health and the Home Office have more to do in ensuring that SHAs, PCTs and Police Authorities fully understand their responsibilities and statutory duties to provide appropriate and effective local services for children in need. Furthermore, all partners in Children's Trusts will need support from central government to develop a local performance framework and minimum data sets in order that their performance can be assessed against the identified needs of local children and young people.

Recommendations

The Government should introduce new statutory targets for safeguarding and child protection alongside the existing statutory attainment and early years targets as quickly as possible. The National Indicator Set should be revised with new national indicators for safeguarding and child protection developed for inclusion in Local Area Agreements for the next Comprehensive Spending Review.

The Department of Health must clarify and strengthen the responsibilities of Strategic Health Authorities for the performance management of Primary Care Trusts on safeguarding and child protection. Formalised and explicit performance indicators should be introduced for Primary Care Trusts.

Regional leadership – Government Offices

2.6 Children and Learners Teams in Government Offices support the implementation of *The Children's Plan*[27] and the *Every Child Matters* programme, the negotiation of LAAs and the translation of national children's policy into local delivery. Children and Learner Teams also have a role in supporting improvement within their region, overseeing the implementation of Serious Case Review Recommendations and challenging the performance of local authorities. The majority of contributors to this progress report recognised the input that they received from Government Offices. However, some also felt that Government Office teams were not always able to provide the level of support or expertise that local areas often need, particularly on complex child protection issues. There is a stronger role for Government Offices to play in raising the profile and increasing the momentum on child protection work. There must be a particular focus on their role in challenging performance and sharing learning and expertise at a regional level. In undertaking this work, Government Offices should ensure that they are joining up sufficiently with all of the other contributors in the region with an interest in the children's safeguarding agenda. Government Office Directors for Children and Learners will wish to ensure that they have the required expertise in child protection within their teams to carry out this role effectively.

Local political leadership

2.7 All local authorities must by now have a designated councillor to act as Lead Member for Children's Services, with responsibility for promoting the safety and welfare of children across all agencies in their area. The sustained commitment from both the Council Leader and the Lead Member for Children's Services is essential if the profile and importance of safeguarding and promoting the welfare of children is to be understood throughout the authority and the Children's Trust. However, it appears that the degree of focus of Council Leaders and Lead Members on safeguarding children from harm is variable. At best there are examples of Lead Members who actively hold Children's Trust partners to account and who deliberately seek to understand the range of service provision in their area. However, such good practice is not yet well established in every local authority.

27 HM Government (DCSF), *The Children's Plan: building brighter futures* (December 2007)

2.8   In order to be most effective, Lead Members must have access to an appropriate level of up-to-date detail of safeguarding practice for their authority, including an understanding of the profile of children and young people in their area, the level of need, and the quality and effectiveness of the services that protect children from harm. They should receive regular reports from the Director for Children's Services (DCS) on service delivery and local outcomes for children and young people, and maintain regular contact with the senior managers of other safeguarding partners. They should provide regular scrutiny of key management information, including assessment and inspection reports, and assure themselves that appropriate quality assurance systems are in place. To support Lead Members in this complex and challenging role, regular training will be required to develop and maintain their knowledge base and enable them, where necessary, to better scrutinise and challenge service delivery to children and young people. The DCSF has recently completed a consultation on the roles of the DCS and Lead Member for Children's Services following the initiatives set out in the DCSF's Children's Plan, with a focus on prevention. The results of this will be published shortly and will be invaluable in shaping their responsibilities more effectively.

Local professional leadership and accountability

2.9   In recent months there has been a great deal of attention on the role of the DCS in safeguarding children, sometimes at the expense of recognising the importance of the role of the local authority Chief Executive. This was underlined by the Society of Local Authority Chief Executives and Senior Managers (SOLACE) in their written evidence to this report, which stated:

"Decision making about the rights of parents and the needs of children, we submit, is the most onerous of local government responsibilities."

2.10 The time is long past when the most junior employee should carry the heaviest burden of accountability. The performance and effectiveness of the most senior managers in each of these services should be assessed against the quality of the outcomes for the most vulnerable children and young people.

2.11 Beyond the local authority, the Children Act 2004 placed a duty to cooperate on each of the key services. It is therefore important that senior managers in partner agencies such as Chief Executives of PCTs and senior police officers work to ensure priority is given to safeguarding children and provide equal commitment, including resources, to local safeguarding partnerships. At senior level there should be a culture of mutual challenge, improvement and openness. Local areas may want to publish an annual report on their safeguarding practice as a way to raise the profile of safeguarding children within both agencies and the local community.

2.12 Attention by senior managers to the quality of services delivered at the front door of each agency, where referrals are received and the risk of harm assessed, is vitally important. Managers must lead by example by taking a personal and visible interest in frontline delivery. They must assure themselves that the assessment of risk of harm to each child and young person is being undertaken effectively and that the referral and assessment processes in *Working Together to Safeguard Children* are being followed intelligently and effectively. Senior managers should be confident that decision making, communication and information sharing within and between each of the local services is effective in keeping children safe even when those services are under pressure. In turn, they should support and value first-line managers ensuring that management oversight of decision making is rigorous and that the lines of communication between senior managers and frontline child protection staff are as short and effective as possible.

> ### Recommendation
>
> Directors of Children's Services, Chief Executives of Primary Care Trusts, Police Area Commanders and other senior service managers must regularly review all points of referral where concerns about a child's safety are received to ensure they are sound in terms of the quality of risk assessments, decision making, onward referrals and multi-agency working.

Directors of Children's Services

2.13 Directors of Children's Services (DCSs) are locally at the centre of safeguarding children, although their remit is far wider, with responsibility for education, children's social care, early years provision and other services to support children and families. There is no doubt that bringing these services together under one local authority department has provided a more integrated approach to support children. But it must be recognised that balancing the many different demands of the role requires significant levels of determination and leadership skills. The responsibility of the role should not be underestimated, nor should the dedication that DCSs show daily in ensuring that children in need receive appropriate services, and, when necessary, adequate protection. The creation of Children's Services Departments has meant that a large proportion of DCSs do not have first-hand experience of frontline social work. It is therefore essential that someone within the senior management team is able to scrutinise cases properly and challenge practice from a position of skill and expertise. However, the DCS should also develop sufficient personal knowledge and understanding of safeguarding and child protection. The development programme for DCSs that the Secretary of State for Children, Schools and Families has recently commissioned from the National College for School Leadership should provide useful extra support in dealing with the complexity of their safeguarding responsibilities.

2.14 Every DCS needs a skilled and well-motivated team to support them, but service delivery is equally dependent on the skills and dedication of frontline staff. DCSs, therefore, need to pay particular attention to the capacity of their frontline workforce. Chapter 4 provides more detail on concerns about the morale of frontline social workers that is resulting in recruitment and retention problems in many areas and ultimately is risking the safety of children. No national workforce strategy will resolve these issues without the robust, decisive and effective leadership of a DCS committed to creating a supportive culture for children's services. It is important to recognise the stressful and emotional content of social work and to create an environment that enables social workers to share their feelings and anxieties without being labelled as inadequate. There is a need for DCSs to put measures in place to help staff deal with the emotional stress of child protection work. Such support needs to be reinforced by a system of good line management that is creative, empowering and sensitive to the individual needs of frontline staff, yet confident enough to set and secure high standards of delivery.

Recommendations

All Directors of Children's Services who do not have direct experience or background in safeguarding and child protection must appoint a senior manager within their team with the necessary skills and experience.

The Department for Children, Schools and Families should organise regular training on safeguarding and child protection and on effective leadership for all senior political leaders and managers across frontline services.

Children's Trusts

2.15 Children's Trusts Boards (rather than the local authority alone) will shortly be required by legislation to undertake a needs analysis, including safeguarding, to inform the development of new Children and Young People's Plans (CYPPs) that come into effect from April 2011. However, it is not clear that the quality of the analyses underpinning current CYPPs is of a consistently high level nationally to drive the resourcing of services to meet the needs of all children. Further work should now be done, at local, regional and national levels, to improve the quality of data on levels of need amongst children and young people, and local authorities should formally reconsider the adequacy of their budgetary commitment. This should include ensuring that management information fully reflect the needs of all those for whom a local authority has responsibilities, up to 18 for most children and 25 for care leavers. A more determined commitment to universal preventative services will facilitate the identification of children in need. Robust information systems need to be in place locally to improve this information. The needs analysis for the CYPP should draw on the data of all partner agencies, and include information about the impact on children and young people of domestic violence, adult alcohol and drug dependency, and adult mental health difficulties.

Recommendation

Every Children's Trust should ensure that the needs assessment that informs their Children and Young People's Plan regularly reviews the needs of all children and young people in their area, paying particular attention to the general need of children and those in need of protection. The National Safeguarding Delivery Unit should support Children's Trusts with this work. Government Offices should specifically monitor and challenge Children's Trusts on the quality of this analysis.

SUPPORT FOR CHILDREN

"When I approach a child, he inspires in me two sentiments: tenderness for what he is, and respect for what he may become."

Louis Pasteur[28]

Focus on the child

3.1   *Every Child Matters* is intended to organise services and resources around children to ensure their safety and proper development, and improve their well-being. However, there are significant levels of concern that current practice, and in particular the pressure of high case-loads for children's social workers and health visitors, has meant that staff often do not have the time needed to maintain effective contact with children, young people and their families in order to achieve positive outcomes. In these circumstances professionals can find it very difficult to take the time to assess the family environment through the eyes of a child or young person. The failure to see the situation from their perspective and to talk to them was highlighted in Ofsted's first annual report of evaluations of Serious Case Reviews.[29] Staff across frontline services need appropriate support and training to ensure that as far as possible they put themselves in the place of the child or young person and consider first and foremost how the situation must feel for them. They need to be able to notice signs of distress in children of all ages, but particularly amongst very young children who are not able to voice concerns and for whom bedwetting, head-banging and other signs may well be a cry for help.

28 Louis Pasteur (1822–95), French chemist and microbiologist
29 Ofsted, *Learning lessons, taking action: Ofsted's evaluations of serious case reviews 1 April 2007 to 31 March 2008* (December 2008)

"It seems like they have to do all this form filling, their bosses' bosses make them do it, but it makes them forget about us."

Boy, 16

"She does things by text book, she doesn't know me as a person."

Girl, 16[30]

Demanding excellence for children

3.2   At the autumn DCSF regional conferences on child deaths and Serious Case Reviews, the University of East Anglia presented early findings from their work on the overview report of Serious Case Reviews initiated during the period 2005–07. They identified that professionals have a "tendency towards justification and reassurance that all was well, rather than more objective consideration and investigation of what had occurred", and that sympathy for parents can lead to the expectations being set too low.[31] Every professional coming into contact with a child in whatever context should be clear that it is not acceptable to do nothing when a child may be in need of help. It is important that the social work relationship, in particular, is not misunderstood as being a relationship for the benefit of the parents or for the relationship itself, rather than a focused intervention to protect the child and promote their welfare.

Early intervention

3.3   Early intervention is vital – not only in ensuring that fewer and fewer children grow up in abusive or neglectful homes, but also to help as many children as possible reach their full potential. The Government's investment in prevention and early intervention, especially through children's centres and extended schools, has been widely welcomed. The Audit Commission has estimated that, if effective early intervention had been provided for just one in ten of those young people sentenced to custody each year, public services alone could have saved over £100 million annually.[32]

30 Quotations taken from findings of research with children undertaken by 11 Million in January 2009 specifically for this report

31 Extract from the presentation of early findings from the overview of Serious Case Reviews during 2005–07, at the recent DCSF regional seminars on child deaths and Serious Case Reviews (University of East Anglia, 2008)

32 HM Treasury, *Policy review of children and young people: A discussion paper* (January 2007)

A recent report co-authored by MPs Graham Allen and Iain Duncan Smith highlights the need for early intervention, noting that "child poverty and income are only part of the picture. Building human capabilities is at least as important and rewarding. Capable, competent human beings will almost always find their way in life, find work and raise happy families." The report also highlights the importance of the first years of a child's life and how they lay the foundation for that child's growth and development; the authors believe that "medical evidence points overwhelmingly in favour of a shift to Early Intervention. It highlights the essential importance of years 0–3 in human development, and the vital influence on years 0–3 of their primary caregivers. That in turn makes it essential to prepare children of 0–18 for their future role as parents. Skills that for generations were passed on, almost unconsciously, now have to be taught: if they are not, we will all reap the consequences."

Graham Allen MP and Rt Hon Iain Duncan Smith MP, *Early Intervention: Good Parents, Great Kids, Better Citizens* (Centre for Social Justice/Smith Institute, 2008)

3.4　However, there are differing understandings (particularly amongst professionals in universal services) about what early intervention actually is – from pre-natal assessment to support for children before they require a child protection plan. Early intervention certainly should not be seen as something that applies only to babies and toddlers. Teenagers who are starting to disengage from school or show signs of anti-social behaviour can also benefit from preventative and early help and support. Schools, youth workers and other professionals should be aware of the signs and know how best to respond.

3.5　Schools and early years settings play a key role in early identification, intervention and support for children at risk of significant harm or who have additional needs. In the findings of the DCSF biennial overview report of Serious Case Reviews from 2003–05,[33] it was found that 68 per cent of the children aged 4 and over who subsequently died or experienced significant harm had been showing signs of poor school attendance. The commitment in the recent 21st Century

33 Brandon, Marion, Pippa Belderson, Catherine Warren, David Howe, Ruth Gardner, Jane Dodsworth, Jane Black, *Analysing Child Deaths and Serious Injury though Abuse – What can we Learn? A Biennial Analysis of Serious Case Reviews 2003-05,* HM Government (2008)

Schools strategy[34] to create a clear national framework for early intervention is timely. Schools and early years settings need to be encouraged to prioritise safeguarding children within their school improvement plans. The inspection and improvement regime for schools needs to ensure that schools are proactively involved in safeguarding children, for example by offering multi-agency services on-site, making sure that their staff understand the referral arrangements in their area, and by continuing involvement in supporting children by attending child protection conferences and sharing information where appropriate. This is crucial in keeping children safe and often in keeping them in education.

Recommendation

Ofsted should revise the inspection and improvement regime for schools giving greater prominence to how well schools are fulfilling their responsibilities for child protection.

Front door – safe and welcoming

3.6   A key factor in identifying children and young people who need help is ensuring services are designed to encourage contact from members of the public, parents and children and young people as well as by other agencies. If safeguarding children is everybody's responsibility, then everybody should know how, and who, to contact if they are concerned about a child or young person. All service providers must look critically at how they receive referrals, the point known as their 'front door'. In local authorities where callers are directed to call centres that handle a wide range of local authority business, the local authority must ensure that any call relating to the protection of a child or young person is quickly transferred to a trained person with immediate access to an experienced social worker allocated to work with that team for more complex or high-risk referrals.

34 HM Government (DCSF), *21st Century Schools: A World-Class Education for Every Child* (December 2008)

Case study A

A common approach to managing referral and assessment

One local authority has been successful in developing an effective and responsive referral system for children and young people. It has been a priority to organise good responses to information about vulnerable children and they have now achieved the basic aim of 'never doing nothing'. The stories at the 'front door' are now managed well and there are consistent responses to what are often chaotic and complex referrals. Central to this way of working are some basic questions:

- What is the nature of the information?

- Who is giving the information?

- How are referrals progressed and who is accountable?

– and three basic principles:

- *Precision* – making sure there is a transparent process (consistently applied) for establishing the cause for concern/referral

- *Visibility* of action in order that every professional in the team knows what is happening and can track progress of the referral

- *Accountability* – making sure that there is a supervisor constantly assessing the decisions being made and the action being taken

This new approach which enables both managers and practitioners to view the whole system as it responds to the identified needs of children and their families is resulting in important and positive results which include:

- increased professional confidence and competence in managing and responding to complex referrals

- consistent and transparent management of referrals across a large county area

- reduced uncertainty amongst referring professionals who always get a response to their referral

- releasing resources both for more preventative work (pre-front door) and for direct work with children and families about whom there are serious concerns

Most importantly, these new practices have ensured that 'doing nothing' is no longer an option. The increased precision and focus which is applied to managing referral information is creating a confidence amongst local professionals that children are safer and resources are targeted where the risk of harm to children and young people is assessed as being the greatest. It is now hoped that this approach can be expanded across the Yorkshire and the Humber region.

Recommendation

The Department for Children, Schools and Families should revise *Working Together to Safeguard Children* to set out clear expectations at all points where concerns about a child's safety are received, ensuring intake/duty teams have sufficient training and expertise to take referrals and that staff have immediate, on-site support available from an experienced social worker. Local authorities should take appropriate action to implement these changes.

Accident and Emergency

3.7   In many of the cases where a child has experienced significant harm or died as a result of abuse, the child has at some point been taken to the Accident and Emergency department of a hospital. *Working Together to Safeguard Children* is helpful in setting out the expectation that "staff in accident and emergency, ambulatory care units, walk-in centres and minor injury units, should be able to recognise abuse and be familiar with local procedures for making enquiries to find out whether a child is subject to a child protection plan". It also recognises the risk that parents may deliberately use different sources of help to conceal repeated injuries to a child or siblings. However, not all Accident and Emergency departments follow this guidance effectively or are yet fully involved in local arrangements for child protection or have easy, up-to-date access to the names of children subject to a child protection plan and the knowledge of whether a child has recently presented at another Accident and Emergency department. All staff in Accident and Emergency departments should be trained to recognise abuse and neglect, with someone available at all times who has up-to-date information on children subject to a child protection plan and what further action should be taken to protect that child. Staff should not work on the assumption that this is the child's first presentation at Accident and Emergency or rely on the parent or carer's assertion that that is the case unless they know this to be true.

3.8   Where medical staff suspect that the injury is non-accidental they must ensure that children's social care services and the child's general practitioner (GP) are notified as soon as possible. Having asked for the parent's permission, they should arrange for a more thorough medical examination of the child in these cases, to identify any additional injuries or concerns. Full notes should be taken and information shared with the social worker. Medical professionals should notify children's social care services and the child's GP of any refusal. No child should be discharged from hospital where medical staff have remaining concerns about that child's safety or welfare. Any concerns they have should be fully explored as set out in Recommendation 19 (see page 86).

Recommendation

The Department of Health and the Department for Children, Schools and Families must strengthen current guidance and put in place the systems and training so that staff in Accident and Emergency departments are able to tell if a child has recently presented at any Accident and Emergency department and if a child is the subject of a Child Protection Plan. If there is any cause for concern, staff must act accordingly, contacting other professionals, conducting further medical examinations of the child as appropriate and necessary, and ensuring no child is discharged whilst concerns for their safety or well-being remain.

Assessment processes

3.9   Fundamental to establishing the extent of a child's need is a child-centred, sensitive and comprehensive assessment. Assessment should involve gathering a full understanding of what is happening to a child in the context of their family circumstances and the wider community, using a variety of sources of information. It must, therefore, be a joint or parallel assessment with all professionals concerned for the child's safety and welfare. Time needs to be spent making sense of this information involving the family where appropriate. Assessment processes should build up an increasingly clear understanding of a child's situation over time, building up a picture of continuous neglect or cumulative concerns about abuse where this exists. This should minimise the risk of repeated initial assessments not taking account of what has gone before. Whilst these principles are well embedded in some services, evidence to this report suggests there is further work to be done to ensure sound assessment processes are in place in every service.

Recommendation

Children's Trusts must ensure that all assessments of need for children and their families include evidence from all the professionals involved in their lives, take account of case histories and significant events (including previous assessments) and above all must include direct contact with the child.

A continuum of support for children

3.10 Local authorities have a general duty to safeguard and promote the welfare of children in need in their area.[35] This is because, for the vast majority of children, the best place for them to be brought up is with their families. Local authorities are required to provide a range and quantity of services appropriate to the needs of children who are 'in need' because they are unlikely to achieve or maintain a reasonable standard of health or development, or whose development is likely to be impaired without support, or who are disabled. This is deliberately a wide definition to ensure every child receives the support needed to stay with his or her family and to secure their proper development. But where the local authority has reasonable cause to believe that a child is suffering or is likely to suffer significant harm the authority must ensure that enquiries are undertaken to make an informed decision about how the safety and welfare of that child is best protected, and take appropriate action to do so.

3.11 In recent years the term 'threshold' has been increasingly used amongst professionals in children's services and their partner agencies. Thresholds are an attempt to limit access to services either because of finance or staffing constraints. Thresholds have no statutory basis and are not part of the *Framework for the Assessment of Children in Need and their Families*.[36] Despite this, concerns have been raised from across the full

35 Under Section 17 of the Children Act 1989
36 Department of Health, April 2000

range of services contributing to this report that thresholds, which act as gateways to restrict services for children, are inconsistent, and are too high. As a result local authorities are missing opportunities to intervene and support families at an earlier stage and avoid situations progressing on a downward spiral. This undermines the very purpose of Section 17 of the Children's Act 1989, which is to provide early support to children and families and prevent the escalation of risk which can lead to a child being harmed. Local authorities that adopt very high threshold criteria run the risk of legal challenge. Children who fall just short of needing a child protection plan are placed at particular risk of suffering harm when services are not provided for them. Local authorities must address this issue urgently and ensure they are providing the range and level of services and support that children in need require. Where this is done well, both statutory and voluntary partners are involved in service planning to ensure that they understand the services that are available to children when making referrals.

3.12   In providing services under the Children Act 1989 it is important that local authorities do not take a compartmentalised view of the legislative framework for meeting the needs of children. If a child is identified as being 'in need', their circumstances should be monitored to ensure they do not change for the worse placing them at risk of significant harm. There should be constant monitoring of the progress of children in need by all agencies involved with the family. Where children are supported at home, the child protection plan must clearly identify the objectives to be achieved, with timescales, that signal either the withdrawal of support to the family or, if the objectives are not achieved, indicate the point when further action must be taken. This is particularly important in cases of child neglect where often there is no single event that 'triggers' matters escalating to an application for a court order. In such cases parents may, or may not, be cooperating and the extent of the risk of harm to the child may increase over time. Realistic timescales need to be applied for these cases to ensure a child is not subjected to long-term neglect. Signs of non-compliance by parents, or indeed threat or manipulation, must form part of the decision to protect a child.

Recommendation

Local authorities must ensure that 'Children in Need', as defined by Section 17 of the Children Act 1989, have early access to effective specialist services and support to meet their needs.

3.13 Social workers should be confident in using the full range of legal options, as appropriate, to safeguard a child's welfare. This includes child assessment orders, care and supervision orders, emergency protection orders and voluntary agreement by parents for their child to be accommodated by the local authority. They must use these options appropriately and decisively. For example, local authorities must consider how appropriate it is to accommodate children with the voluntary agreement of their parents,[37] which can be revoked at any time, when there are concerns for a child's safety. They should be ready to act decisively if it becomes necessary to apply for a care order.

Evidence-based programmes

3.14 Vulnerable children and families have a right to expect that the services they are provided with are based on evidence that they have been shown to work in meeting their needs. There have been a number of examples of evidence-based programmes that practitioners and service leaders have found particularly supportive in their contributions to this report. Family Nurse Partnerships, that provide intensive support for the most vulnerable first time parents, have proven benefits with evaluations stretching over 25 years in the US and seem to have been well received here. The announcement of the expansion of this service in the recent Children's Health Strategy *Healthy lives, brighter futures*[38] is welcome. Family Intervention Programmes have introduced new ways to support parents at times when their relationships come under strain, and give more support to children when family relationships break down. Parenting programmes already being used widely include Webster Stratton, Strengthening Families, and Triple P, all of which have been shown to be particularly effective for younger children. Three other programmes – Functional Family Therapy, Multi-systemic Therapy and Multidimensional Treatment Foster Care – are currently being piloted in some local authorities in England and have the potential to deliver positive outcomes. DCSF, the National Safeguarding Delivery Unit and existing organisations who work to share good practice in safeguarding children all have a role to play in sharing the learning from evidence-based programmes and encouraging their availability.

---

37 Under Section 20 of the Children Act 1989
38 HM Government (DCSF and Department of Health), *Healthy lives, brighter futures – The strategy for children and young people's health* (2009)

Reflective practice

3.15 The role of social work staff and managers is particularly critical in ensuring enabling action to protect children. There is concern that the tradition of deliberate, reflective social work practice is being put in danger because of an overemphasis on process and targets, resulting in a loss of confidence amongst social workers. It is vitally important that social work is carried out in a supportive learning environment that actively encourages the continuous development of professional judgement and skills. Regular, high-quality, organised supervision is critical, as are routine opportunities for peer-learning and discussion. Currently, not enough time is dedicated to this and individuals are carrying too much personal responsibility, with no outlet for the sometimes severe emotional and psychological stresses that staff involved in child protection often face. Supervision should be open and supportive, focusing on the quality of decisions, good risk analysis, and improving outcomes for children rather than meeting targets.

Recommendations

The Social Work Task Force should establish guidelines on guaranteed supervision time for social workers that may vary depending on experience.

The Department for Children, Schools and Families should revise *Working Together to Safeguard Children* to set out the elements of high quality supervision focused on case planning, constructive challenge and professional development.

Data systems

3.16 There are definite advantages to electronic record keeping in place of the previous often inaccessible paper files. Technology offers the potential for professionals to share information more effectively, to make information more accessible, and to use systems to manage the workflow of children's services. The new ContactPoint system will have particular advantages in reducing the possibility of children for whom there are concerns going unnoticed.

3.17 Practitioners and managers are committed to the principle of an electronic system and have no desire to return to paper-based case management. However, the current state of the technology – particularly the local IT systems that support the use of the Integrated

Children's System (ICS) – is hampering progress. Professional practice and judgement, as said by many who contributed evidence to this report, are being compromised by an over-complicated, lengthy and tick-box assessment and recording system. The direct interaction and engagement with children and their families, which is at the core of social work, is said to be at risk as the needs of a work management tool overtake those of evidence-based assessment, sound analysis and professional judgement about risk of harm.

3.18 There is no single national IT system that delivers the ICS requirements. Some areas have access to systems that support practice, but there is wide variation from area to area in the time staff spend inputting information into the ICS. Local authorities that ensured practice strongly informed the implementation process appear to have been successful in reducing time spent by social workers in front of screens. Those local authorities with strong leadership and a confident workforce ensure social workers remain primarily focused upon contact with children and families. However, there remain fundamental limitations to local systems that impact daily on the working lives of many social workers and, as a result, affect the quality of their work with children and their families. Some of the concerns shared by contributors to this report are detailed below. Local authorities are having to find ways to work around their systems – often introducing parallel systems for capturing qualitative data – with the result that the benefits of the system are being undermined. Too much time and money is being spent at local level trying to correct the failings of individual systems and stronger national leadership of ICS is needed.

> **Examples of concerns about ICS raised in evidence**
>
> - The systems do not support reflective thinking and risk analysis
> - Some of the systems in use require some data to be re-entered for each child in a family
> - Some of the systems in use do not allow qualitative assessments and case notes to be captured
> - Most systems do not produce chronologies that can be used in court, although the specification published in June 2008 requires this
> - It is hard to use the outputs to engage with children and families

Case study B

Integrated Children's System

One local authority has implemented an ICS which is supporting improvement in the overall management and delivery of children's services. It is acknowledged that there are still improvements to be made, but it is also clear that this would indeed be the case where any system is being developed to support children and their families. Critical to their local success in implementation is:

- a clear and open relationship from the start with the developer/ provider of the system

- a local dedicated IT team who understand the needs of the children's service and who can broker this with the developers of the system

- senior leadership involvement in the commissioning and ongoing development of the system

- a commitment throughout the service to focusing on practice and not exclusively timescales. The quality of assessments and decision making is reinforced at all times

- recognition that the multi-disciplinary relationships around the system must be in place and be effective for the system to work. Where this is the case, good information sharing amongst professionals will be replicated in the system

- clarity amongst staff that ICS is not a replacement for professional judgement but rather a tool to enable and support case-load planning and management and multi-disciplinary working

Recommendations

The Department for Children, Schools and Families should undertake a feasibility study with a view to rolling out a single national Integrated Children's System better able to address the concerns identified in this report, or find alternative ways to assert stronger leadership over the local systems and their providers. This study should be completed within six months of this report.

Whether or not a national system is introduced, the Department for Children, Schools and Families should take steps to improve the utility of the Integrated Children's System, in consultation with social workers and their managers, to be effective in supporting them in their role and their contact with children and families, partners, services and courts, and to ensure appropriate transfer of essential information across organisational boundaries.

3.19 Irrespective of the methods used for recording and managing casework, local leaders must ensure that children and young people's information is managed and recorded effectively to reduce their risk of harm. Clearly systems are only as good as the information put into them, and the priority should be to ensure that staff are able to dedicate maximum efforts to face-to-face contact with children and families.

INTERAGENCY WORKING

"Relationships are crucial; it's not about structures, it's about making it work out there for children."

Social worker

4.1   It is clear that most staff in social work, youth work, education, police, health and other frontline services are committed to the principle of interagency working, and recognise that children can only be protected effectively when all agencies pool information, expertise and resources so that a full picture of the child's life is better understood. Cooperative working is increasingly becoming the normal way of working. However, good examples of joint working too often rely on the goodwill of individuals. Colleagues in education, early years, health and police are vital partners in protecting children and they need to be willing and proactive in discharging their statutory duty to cooperate on child safeguarding.

"*Some agencies still think they are helping out social care rather than thinking that safeguarding is everybody's responsibility.*" Local Safeguarding Children Board (LSCB) Chair, Loughborough University 2009 LSCB Survey [39]

4.2   The Government's *Working Together to Safeguard Children* set out sound principles and procedures for collaborative working, but to protect children these need to be intelligently and effectively applied in every local service. All professionals working with a child should explicitly understand their responsibilities in order to achieve positive outcomes, keep children safe, and complement the support that other professionals may be providing. They should all know when a child is subject to a child protection plan and act accordingly.

39 Interim findings to be published in spring 2009: Loughborough University research led by Professor Alan France and Emily Munro

Recommendations

The Department for Children, Schools and Families must strengthen *Working Together to Safeguard Children*, and Children's Trusts must take appropriate action to ensure:

- all referrals to children's services from other professionals lead to an initial assessment, including direct involvement with the child or young person and their family, and the direct engagement with, and feedback to, the referring professional;

- core group meetings, reviews and casework decisions include all the professionals involved with the child, particularly police, health, youth services and education colleagues. Records must be kept which must include the written views of those who cannot make such meetings; and

- formal procedures are in place for managing a conflict of opinions between professionals from different services over the safety of a child.

4.3   Yet it is evident that the challenges of working across organisational boundaries continue to pose barriers in practice, and that cooperative efforts are often the first to suffer when services and individuals are under pressure. Examples of poor practice highlighted to this report include child protection conferences where not all the services involved in a child's life are present or able to give a view; or where one professional disagrees with a decision and their view is not explored in more detail; and repeated examples of professionals not receiving feedback on referrals. As a result of each of these failures, children or young people at risk of neglect or abuse will be exposed to greater danger. The referring professional may also be left with ongoing anxiety and concern about the child or young person. This needs to be addressed if all local services are to be effective in keeping children and young people safe.

Recommendations

All police, probation, adult mental health and adult drug and alcohol services should have well understood referral processes which prioritise the protection and well-being of children. These should include automatic referral where domestic violence or drug or alcohol abuse may put a child at risk of abuse or neglect.

The National Safeguarding Delivery Unit should urgently develop guidance on referral and assessment systems for children affected by domestic violence, adult mental health problems, and drugs and alcohol misuse using current best practice. This should be shared with local authorities, health and police with an expectation that the assessment of risk and level of support given to such children will improve quickly and significantly in every Children's Trust.

The Department for Children, Schools and Families should establish statutory representation on Local Safeguarding Children Boards from schools, adult mental health and adult drug and alcohol services.

Adult and child services working together

4.4   It is estimated at least 200,000 children live in households where there is a known high risk case of domestic abuse and violence, with very many more affected at some point in time.[40] Approximately 450,000 parents[41] are estimated to have mental health problems; an estimated 250,000 – 350,000 children[42] have parents who are problematic drug users, and around 1.3 million children[43] live with parents who are thought to misuse alcohol. In this context, it is vital that professional staff working with adults are trained to identify and assess the needs of, and risk of harm to, children and young people. These issues are a consistent feature of Serious Case Reviews,[44] demonstrating how seriously they put children at risk of significant harm. There are some

40 Figures provided by Co-ordinated Action Against Domestic Abuse (CAADA)
41 Morris, J and M Wates, 'Supporting Disabled Parents and Parents with Additional Support Needs' in *Adult's Services Knowledge Review 11* (Social Care Institute for Excellence, 2006)
42 Advisory Council on the Misuse of Drugs, *Hidden Harm: Responding to the Needs of Problem Drug Users* (2003)
43 Prime Minister's Strategy Unit, *Alcohol Harm Reduction Project – Interim Analytical Report* (2003)
44 Brandon, Marion, Pippa Belderson, Catherine Warren, David Howe, Ruth Gardner, Jane Dodsworth, Jane Black, *Analysing Child Deaths and Serious Injury though Abuse – What can we Learn? A Biennial Analysis of Serious Case Reviews 2003–05,* HM Government (2008)

examples of good practice of adult and children's services working together to ensure that the protection of children is paramount in contact with adults. However, there are too many examples of referral and assessment processes that do not adequately identify and assess the risk of harm to children or take the necessary action to support those children.

4.5   These are complicated matters and they need to be handled with great care. It is vital to ensure that, in creating a robust system of identifying and supporting these children appropriately, crude systems of referral are not used that deter victims of domestic violence or those suffering with mental health illness from seeking help, for fear that this would automatically put in jeopardy their right to care for their child. Sound referral systems must be based on proper assessment and judgement. The answer must lie in joint working between police, health and children's services to ensure that the risk of harm to children is well understood, assessed and acted upon as appropriate in every case. Local areas need further support in consistently developing such robust arrangements, and the National Safeguarding Delivery Unit should address this as one of its earliest priorities.

Case study C
Multi-agency working – *an example from one local authority*

In one local authority, doing the 'basics' well has enabled the Local Safeguarding Children Board (LSCB) to develop a strong and mature partnership. The LSCB benefits from a personal commitment from Executive Directors across each of the health trusts. Four Health Trusts (two acute, one mental health and one Primary Care Trust (PCT) have their own safeguarding boards which meet quarterly, and are led by their respective Executive Directors. The function of the health safeguarding boards is to co-ordinate safeguarding practice across the trusts, ensuring a 'two way learning and improvement dialogue' with the LSCB. These arrangements also support an annual event to consider cross boundary issues, across the trusts and two local authority areas. This has led to implementation of the same protocols regardless of the local authority area where a child or family live.

One trust has recently established an operational multi-agency safeguarding team across children and adult services. There are weekly multi-disciplinary case review meetings with partners and multi-agency audits. The Accident and Emergency department holds a weekly psycho-social meeting, to discuss attendances in the previous week with representation from hospital and social care staff. Robust screening is universally applied for safeguarding issues including domestic violence, all attendances at hospital are notified to the health visitor, school nurse, GP, and social worker, and a rigorous risk assessment is undertaken before any child is discharged.

Vulnerable children are 'flagged' in GP practices, there is a named safeguarding GP in each practice, and there is also a GP with a special interest in safeguarding contributing to the PCT's strategic safeguarding work and acting as a key conduit to GP practices. Regular training is provided by designated and named professionals to GPs to maximise their contribution to the safeguarding agenda.

Health Trusts are represented on the seven sub-committees of the LSCB, which enables them to influence any training programmes, identify likely barriers to change, and exploit the full impact of interagency working. The value of interagency audit has been particularly important in driving change and creating a culture of continuous improvement.

Information sharing

4.6   Despite the fact that the Government gave clear guidance on information sharing in 2006 and updated it in October 2008,[45] there continues to be a real concern across all sectors, but particularly in the health services, about the risk of breaching confidentiality or data protection law by sharing concerns about a child's safety. The laws governing data protection and privacy are still not well understood by frontline staff or their managers. It is clear that different agencies (and their legal advisers) often take different approaches.

4.7   Whilst the law rightly seeks to preserve individuals' privacy and confidentiality, it should not be used (and was never intended) as a barrier to appropriate information sharing between professionals. The safety and welfare of children is of paramount importance, and

45 HM Government, *Information sharing: Guidance for practitioners and managers* (2008)

agencies may lawfully share confidential information about the child or the parent, without consent, if doing so is in the public interest. A public interest can arise in a wide range of circumstances, including the protection of a child from harm, and the promotion of child welfare. Even where the sharing of confidential medical information is considered inappropriate, it may be proportionate for a clinician to share the fact that they have concerns about a child.

> "The key factors in deciding whether or not to share confidential information are necessity and proportionality, ie whether the proposed sharing is likely to make an effective contribution to preventing the risk and whether the public interest in sharing information overrides the interest in maintaining confidentiality. In making the decision you must weigh up what might happen if the information is shared against what might happen if it is not and make a decision based on professional judgement."
>
> *Information sharing: Guidance for practitioners and managers*
> HM Government (2008)

4.8   Those who have local accountability for keeping children safe should ensure that all staff in every service, from frontline practitioners to legal advisers and managers in statutory services and the voluntary sector, understand the circumstances in which they may lawfully share information about both children and parents, and that it is in the public interest to prioritise the safety and welfare of children. Agencies should regularly test their local information sharing arrangements to satisfy themselves that their procedures are understood and working properly to protect children.

Recommendation

Every Children's Trust should assure themselves that partners consistently apply the Information Sharing Guidance published by the Department for Children, Schools and Families and the Department for Communities and Local Government to protect children.

Common Assessment Framework

4.9   The Common Assessment Framework (CAF) is a tool designed to aid the assessment of a child's needs where more than one practitioner is likely to be involved in meeting those needs. It is designed for the early intervention end of the spectrum of need rather than for children who are at risk of significant harm. It is still too early to make a judgement on the effectiveness of the CAF in improving outcomes for children and young people, and opinion from contributors to this report has been divided. There has been some evidence that the CAF has been helpful in bringing together a wider range of professionals to make joint assessments that are both positive in achieving better assessments of a child and as a learning experience for staff. However, it is in danger, like other tools, of becoming process-focused or, even worse, a barrier to services for children where access to services depends on a completed CAF form. All agencies need further help in using the CAF effectively and consistently. They also need further support in managing the role of lead practitioners to ensure that all those who undertake this role have the time, training and relationships needed to allow them to support children effectively.

Views on CAF from contributors to this Progress Report

"The CAF has made a huge difference in this area to the early identification of children and young people in need."

Local authority managers during a fieldwork visit

"The CAF can be very effective in building bridges and shared understanding between different professional groups."

Police organisation in written evidence

"The CAF has caused a lot of confusion and is burdensome to complete, not least because not all agencies know how to feed their information into it."

Voluntary organisation in written evidence

CHILDREN'S WORKFORCE

"All kids need is a little help, a little hope and somebody who believes in them."

Earvin 'Magic' Johnson[46]

5.1　Few careers are as demanding or rewarding as that of working with children, young people and their families. People who enter the children's workforce, be it in the health services, the police, education, youth work or social work, do so to make a difference to other people's lives. Every day, thousands of children are helped, supported and in some cases have their lives saved by these staff. However, rather than feeling valued for their commitment and expertise professionals across these services often feel undervalued, unsupported and at risk. Morale amongst social workers in services for children is particularly low. There is a desperate need for more health visitors, and many paediatricians and police officers report that child protection work is often of low status in contrast to the challenges that accompany it. As a result, children may be being put at risk of suffering harm.

Progress so far

5.2　The issues facing all the staff working with children remain very real. Vacancies for children's social workers in local authorities stood at 9.5 per cent in 2006, [47] compared with 0.7 per cent for teachers.[48] Turnover rates were also high at 9.6 per cent. 64 per cent of local authorities reported difficulties in recruiting children's social workers in 2008, and 39 per cent had difficulty in retaining them, although progress has been made since 2006.[49] In some authorities visited in

---

46 Earvin 'Magic' Johnson (1959 –), US basketball player
47 Children's, Young People's and Families' Social Care Workforce Survey 2006, Local Authority Workforce Intelligence Group
48 618G survey (annual, DCSF), full-time vacancy rate for maintained nursery/primary, secondary and special schools in England
49 Local Government Workforce Survey 2008 (available on line at www.lga.gov.uk/lga/core/page. do?pageId=1095305)

the preparation of this report over half of social workers are newly qualified with less than a year's experience. One survey suggested that nearly three-quarters of children's social workers report that average case-loads have increased since 2003.[50] Equally worryingly, the number of health visitors is at its lowest in 14 years.[51] Research for Community Care as part of the 'Children in Focus' series back in 2002 suggests that working in child protection teams within the police service is seen as being low status.[52] This was a view repeated by a number of police service representatives in the evidence to this Report.

5.3   In December 2008, the Department for Children, Schools and Families (DCSF) published the *2020 Children and Young People's Workforce Strategy*,[53] setting out the Government's vision for all those working with children. Moreover, the Secretary of State for Children, Schools and Families established the Social Work Task Force (SWTF) to focus particularly on the roles of those working in frontline social work services for children and young people. The Workforce Strategy and the SWTF are very welcome responses to the current challenges in social work. They demonstrate a recognition that, whilst there have been significant improvements in some parts of the children's workforce, these have focused primarily on universal services, particularly education, and have not yet reached social workers.

Social workers

5.4   Frontline social workers and social work managers are under an immense amount of pressure. Low staff morale, poor supervision, high case-loads, under-resourcing and inadequate training each contribute to high levels of stress and recruitment and retention difficulties. Many social workers feel the size of the task in protecting children and young people from harm is insurmountable and this increases the risk of harm. Social work and, in particular, child protection work is felt to be a 'Cinderella' service within other parts of the children's workforce. It is noticeable that education has received substantially more investment over the last decade. Public vilification of social workers has a negative effect on staff and has serious implications for the effectiveness, status and morale of the children's workforce as a whole. There has been a long-term appetite in the

50 UNISON, *Still slipping through the net? Frontline staff assess children's safeguarding progress* (2008)

51 Unite/Community Practitioners' and Health Visitors' Association Omnibus Survey, 2008

52 Sally Gillen (available online at www.communitycare.co.uk/Articles/2002/05/23/36528/child-protection-blues.html)

53 HM Government (DCSF), *2020 Children and Young People's Workforce Strategy* (December 2008)

media to portray social workers in ways that are negative and undermining. Inevitably, other ways of helping children, young people and families often look more appealing to staff. However, without highly motivated and confident social workers the reality is that more children will be exposed to harm.

A national supply strategy for social work

5.5   The issues outlined above have resulted in a recruitment and retention crisis within social work. There is a national and local shortage of qualified social workers able and willing to undertake the skilled safeguarding and child protection work required. Many authorities are reliant on agency social workers, despite this being a short-term solution. Together with the high turnover of permanent staff and use of staff from abroad, it fails to provide vulnerable children with the continuity of the same worker with whom they can form a long-term relationship. Good local leadership will not of itself be enough to overcome these issues, although it will play a crucial role.

Case study D
Recruitment and retention of social workers

Managers in one local authority wanted to look at opportunities to improve the recruitment and retention of social workers. A range of innovative and effective solutions have been found.

A strategy has been drawn up, evaluated and the following key points have been identified as important in retaining and recruiting social workers:

- a clear induction programme for new staff with a strong emphasis on development;

- a new 'consultant' role within the organisational structure for experienced social workers to support newly qualified staff, increasing practitioner confidence, skills and assertiveness, and leading to increased direct work with children and families;

- a strong supervision policy where workloads and case management are regularly discussed and assessed;

- a new pilot with a local university to sponsor places on training programmes; and

> - the creation of a joint safeguarding service bringing together staff from three previously separate teams (social care, education and health), emphasising the authority's commitment to integrated working, and including an expert-staffed advice line for professionals.

5.6   DCSF, with support from the SWTF, should develop a strategy to raise the profile of social work and positively seek to overcome the current media and public misunderstandings about the important contribution that social workers make to keeping children safe. It needs to forecast and plan to meet projections for social workers over future years, taking into account the complexity and weight of case-loads, and supervision and training needs. There should be clearer and more attractive entry routes into social work for those unqualified staff who would like to progress into qualified social work roles. Building on work currently being developed by the Children's Workforce Development Council (CWDC), there should also be efforts to engage professionals in mid-career in other sectors to retrain to enter the social care workforce and reward them for doing so. Further consideration needs to be given to how best to retain experienced staff enabling them to continue to be available to work with children and families on the frontline by making effective use of the advanced practitioner status to be introduced later this year. This will not be an easy task or one that comes without a significant financial commitment, but a comparison should be made with the resources provided to achieve similar outcomes in the teaching profession, if safeguarding and child protection services really are to be effective in keeping children safe.

Remodelling social work

5.7   There are similarities between the current pressure, overload and dissatisfaction that many social workers feel, and that of the teaching workforce ten years ago. Case-loads are consistently high, increasing the risk of harm to children and creating anxiety for social workers. The introduction of teaching assistants and advanced skills teachers, protected preparation time and other elements of remodelling have made great strides in overcoming these issues in education.

5.8 Some similar steps, led by CWDC, are now being taken for social workers, with the introduction, for example, of the Newly Qualified Social Worker Status and the development of a career progression framework for social workers. However, there remains a real need for a determined and well-resourced national remodelling strategy for social work. A programme to remodel children's social work could include the introduction of multi-skilled teams with shared ownership of a manageable case-load. Within a team there could be a mix of junior and more experienced social workers along with administrative and multi-disciplinary support. There should be a focus on efficient case management using the skills of all members of the team. This approach, already used in some areas, ensures continuity of service to the child and that social workers are not isolated in their contact with the child and their family, and have others around them with whom they can discuss concerns and make decisions together or undertake joint visits. Skilled administrative support also allows social workers to focus on their areas of expertise, as can other professionals in the team. An effective remodelling programme will ensure that experienced and skilled staff are recognised and motivated, using the role of advanced practitioner due to be introduced later this year, with the importance of their role reflected through a pay structure that is comparable to others with similar skills and experience elsewhere in the children's workforce. Within this context, practitioners, teams and individuals should all have a mixed case-load of both child protection and children in need work. No social worker should handle only the more complex and emotionally demanding child protection cases. The case study on page 50 shares the experience of one local authority that has devised a new arrangement to ensure continuity of help to the families and to support frontline staff. These are issues which many authorities will face and will have varied ways of dealing with.

Case study E
Remodelling social work

"If the people working with children and their families are not competent, then the infrastructure to support them will make no difference or add any value."

Local authority Deputy Director

It is this starting point which led one local authority to 'reclaim social work'. Observing that social work as a profession has lost it way, lacks confidence, expertise and gravitas, is over-bureaucratised and risk averse they suggest that whilst assessment should remain central to planning and decision making, more time should be spent on direct intervention with families to effect positive change. In order to achieve this, they state that clear professional accountability, clinical support and high calibre practitioners are fundamental.

At the heart of the model is the Social Work Unit (SWU). Under the leadership of a consultant social worker (CSW), members of the SWU (a social worker, a children's practitioner, a family therapist and a unit co-ordinator) work to deliver the service.

Key aims of the SWUs are to use systemic approaches and social learning theory interventions to create change in families.

Families and children want consistency and this approach goes a long way to securing that. This requires SWUs to be flexible and responsive in the roles and tasks they undertake.

The CSW has full responsibility for all cases allocated to their SWU.

"If you have excellent social workers, you don't stop them practising. That's why we now have consultant social workers."

Each family, child and young person is known to each member of the SWU. Each SWU meets weekly to agree the tasks needed to be undertaken that week. The families are discussed and tasks are allocated to members of the SWU according to availability, skill, and knowledge of and relationship to the family. Direct work is undertaken by everyone as appropriate (including the CSW). The SWU is given a high degree of autonomy and is expected to take responsibility for the decisions made and the actions taken. All practitioners in the SWUs have delegate authority for some limited financial spend. It operates as a whole. The CSW line manages the social worker and children's practitioner. The Clinician receives clinical supervision and line management from the Supervising Clinicians within Family Support. The SWU co-ordinators are line managed by administration managers within each service area.

This is a new paradigm for social work. The SWUs have to have both a good understanding of evidence-based interventions and at the same time understand and be able to manage risk. At the centre of all the work is to focus on the need to protect children from significant harm.

There is a commitment to creating a culture where good social work thrives. This means reducing the bureaucratic burdens on units and creating a new relationship between CSW and managers.

"No professional social work practitioner or manager gets a job in this authority without being successful at an interview panel always chaired by either the deputy director or assistant director."

In the words of one consultant when talking about a complex case the Unit had worked with, *"I feel the whole family has benefited ... it's enormously satisfying and professionally invigorating"*.

Recommendations

The Social Work Task Force should:

- develop the basis for a national children's social worker supply strategy that will address recruitment and retention difficulties, to be implemented by the Department for Children, Schools and Families. This should have a particular emphasis on child protection social workers;

- work with the Children's Workforce Development Council and other partners to implement, on a national basis, clear progression routes for children's social workers;

- develop national guidelines setting out maximum case-loads of children in need and child protection cases, supported by a weighting mechanism to reflect the complexity of cases, that will help plan the workloads of children's social workers; and

- develop a strategy for remodelling children's social work which delivers shared ownership of cases, administrative support and multi-disciplinary support to be delivered nationally.

Children's Trusts should ensure a named, and preferably co-located, representative from the police service, community paediatric specialist and health visitor are active partners within each children's social work department.

Social work initial training

5.9 The introduction in 2003 of the degree course in social work is widely acknowledged to be a great advance in improving social workers' skills. However, the quality and content of degree courses are not yet sufficiently well developed and there is no rigorous assessment regime in place to ensure that standards are being met by providers. The degree course should ensure social workers are prepared for the realities of working with children and families who may have complex needs and parents who, in some cases, may be intentionally deceptive or manipulative. Social workers themselves do not think that their training is equipping them to take on the responsibilities for which they are being trained – two-thirds of newly qualified social workers felt that the degree prepared them just enough or not at all for their current role.[54]

5.10 At the heart of the difficultly in preparing social workers through a degree course is that, without an opportunity to specialise in child protection work or even in children's social work, students are covering too much ground without learning the skills and knowledge to support any particular client group well. There are few placements offered in children's services and fewer still at the complex end of child protection or children 'in need'. It is currently possible to qualify as a social worker without any experience of child protection, or even of working within a local authority, and to be holding a full case-load of child protection cases immediately upon appointment. The current degree programme should be reformed to allow for specialism after the first year, with no graduate entering frontline children's social work without having completed a specialised degree including a placement within a frontline statutory children's social work team, or having completed further professional development and children's social work experience to build on generic training.

54 Children's Workforce Development Council Research Team, *Newly Qualified Social Workers. A report on consultations with newly qualified social workers, employers and those in higher education* (unpublished preliminary findings)

"I was astonished ... to find that a new graduate is immediately a qualified social worker and can work unsupervised. If you compare that with other professions – medicine or dentistry, optometry, pharmacy, or teaching – they have a period of one or two years during which you go out on placement and acquire, under supervision, the general practical ability and experience that will enable them to practise successfully ... If either a doctor or nurse were going to specialise in work with children, for example, they would need to undergo accredited specialist training, and they would have a mark on the register saying they had such training."

From an interview with Rosie Varley, chair of the General Social Care Council, in *The Guardian* (4 February 2009)

5.11 A specialist children's social work degree would need to provide students with an in-depth understanding of child development as well as more practical skills. Social workers need good observation and analytical skills in order to be able to understand the nature of the relationship between a parent and child, to understand signs of non-compliance, to work alongside a family, and to come to safe and evidence-based judgements about the best course of action. They need to develop the emotional resilience to manage the challenges they will face in dealing with potentially difficult families. They need to know how to record information clearly, present key case information, reflect and analyse on what they are seeing, and to communicate it clearly to colleagues and other professionals. Furthermore, social workers need a thorough understanding of the legal framework surrounding safeguarding and child protection. The social work degree needs to be developed to provide these skills.

Recommendations

The General Social Care Council, together with relevant government departments, should:

- work with higher education institutions and employers to raise the quality and consistency of social work degrees and strengthen their curriculums to provide high quality practical skills in children's social work;

- work with higher education institutions to reform the current degree programme towards a system which allows for specialism in children's social work, including statutory children's social work placements, after the first year; and

- put in place a comprehensive inspection regime to raise the quality and consistency of social work degrees across higher education institutions.

Newly qualified social workers

5.12 Social workers must have guaranteed support and supervision during their first year to enable them to develop their skills and their confidence as a professional in a relatively safe learning environment whilst still having exposure to children in complex and difficult circumstances. CWDC's Newly Qualified Social Worker pilot is currently providing 1,000 new social workers in 90 local authorities with protected time for training and development and better quality, more frequent supervision in their first year of practice. 1,000 more newly qualified social workers will receive this from September. Working with CWDC, the SWTF should take action to ensure that all newly qualified social workers receive this level of support.

Continuing professional development (CPD) for social workers

5.13 This Progress Report has heard much about the complexity and challenges facing frontline staff working with children and families to protect children from harm. No two cases are the same and each case should be considered as a learning opportunity, through which the social worker develops his or her skills and knowledge base. It is important to develop a culture of continuous learning and development as a natural part of social work practice.

5.14   However, in order to carry out their roles effectively, social workers and their managers need access to good quality post-qualifying training. It is particularly important that those working in child protection regularly refresh their skills and knowledge base, ensuring they are fully aware of and competent in undertaking evidence-based, effective assessments and appropriate interventions. There are, however, shortfalls in CPD and post-qualifying training for social workers, together with reticence from employers to release and sponsor staff to take up such opportunities. There is currently no national framework for CPD. Nor are there clear links between CPD and career progression. This impacts upon staff morale and their motivation to remain in post and develop their careers. Training opportunities across local authorities are varied and locally sourced, particularly for first line managers. This should be addressed to ensure social workers have the continuing support to be competent and confident in their roles and managers are able to provide effective oversight of casework and provide high-quality supervision.

5.15   As a first step, a post-graduate qualification in safeguarding children is needed that is practice-based, focusing on the key skills required for effective working with children and families and protecting children from harm. All children's social workers should be expected to complete this postgraduate qualification as soon as is practicable. It will need to be funded centrally and with protected study time made available.

Recommendation

The Department for Children, Schools and Families and the Department for Innovation, Universities and Skills should introduce a fully-funded, practice-focused children's social work postgraduate qualification for experienced children's social workers, with an expectation they will complete the programme as soon as is practicable.

Qualifications for overseas social workers

5.16   There are relatively high numbers of social workers who were trained outside the UK with 6,400[55] registered with the General Social Care Council (GSCC) in 2007 (8 per cent of all social work staff

55 Moriarty, Manthorpe, Hussein and Cornes, *Staff Shortages and Immigration in the Social Care Sector* (a paper prepared for the Migration Advisory Committee, Kings College London (2008))

registered).[56] Their contribution to safeguarding children in the UK is welcomed and valued with many local authorities relying heavily on their contribution and praising the training they have received abroad. Many social workers who qualified overseas take it upon themselves to ensure they are familiar with the safeguarding framework in the UK. However, this training must become consistent for every overseas qualified social worker, as must their English language capability for the minority for whom English is not their first language. The DCSF, together with the GSCC and CWDC, and partners, should explore how this can best be achieved through a national framework of in-house and external training, leading to a conversion qualification.

Recommendation

The Department for Children, Schools and Families, working with the Children's Workforce Development Council, General Social Care Council and partners should introduce a conversion qualification and English language test for internationally qualified children's social workers that ensures understanding of legislation, guidance and practice in England. Consideration should be given to the appropriate length of a compulsory induction period in a practice setting prior to formal registration as a social worker in England.

Training across all agencies

5.17 Training for social workers, police, teachers, health visitors, GPs and paediatricians all have different professional starting points on engaging with children and young people, governed by the nature of the service they provide. Yet it is essential that all professionals working with children have a solid understanding of child development. All those who work with children need to be able to identify the signs that suggest a child may be suffering from abuse or neglect and know what actions to take to safeguard the child's welfare. This would include knowing when a child is not developing as would be expected for their age.

---

56 Not all of these would go on to practise as social workers and only some would become children's social workers

> **Recommendation**
>
> Children's Trusts should ensure that all staff who work with children receive initial training and continuing professional development which enables them to understand normal child development and recognise potential signs of abuse or neglect.

5.18   Multi-agency training is important in helping professionals understand the respective roles and responsibilities and the procedures of each agency involved in child protection, in developing a joint understanding of assessment and decision making practices, and in learning from Serious Case Reviews. However, the scale and quality of multi-agency training needs to be substantially improved to ensure that all those organisations who are part of a child's life, such as early years providers, schools, youth services, health, and the police, social workers, paramedics and others who step in when problems arise, have this understanding.

> **Recommendation**
>
> All Children's Trusts should have sufficient multi-agency training in place to create a shared language and understanding of local referral procedures, assessment, information sharing and decision making across early years, schools, youth services, health, police and other services who work to protect children. A named child protection lead in each setting should receive this training.

5.19   The introduction of the *Common Core of Skills and Knowledge*[57] in 2005 aimed to provide a common language for working with children. However, following concerns about the extent to which the Common Core addresses issues of integrated working; working with families to support vulnerable children and young people; and how well embedded it is in some parts of the workforce such as the health sector or the police, the *2020 Children and Young People's Workforce Strategy* has called for a review, which is welcomed.

Employer and social worker codes of practice

5.20   The GSCC has developed codes of practice for social workers and for their employers which provide the basis for a national 'contract' to develop the profession. However, it appears that the codes are in need of updating to be more effective in protecting children. The *Code of*

57 HM Government, *Common Core of Skills and Knowledge for the Children's Workforce* (2005)

Practice for Social Care Workers should be reviewed to ensure the needs of children are paramount, regardless of whether the social worker is in adult or children's services. The employer code provides an important basis for a national standard for employers, and therefore should be revised to clarify expectations around accountability, quality and amounts of supervision, reflective practice and support, and commitment to staff training and CPD. The employer code should be made statutory for all employers of social workers.

> ## Recommendation
>
> The General Social Care Council should review the Code of Practice for Social Workers and the employers' code ensuring the needs of children are paramount in both and that the employers' code provides for clear lines of accountability, quality supervision and support, and time for reflective practice. The employers' code should then be made statutory for all employers of social workers.

Health professionals

5.21 Health visitors play a key role in child protection, particularly for very young children who are unable to raise the alarm when suffering from abuse or neglect. The evaluation of 161 Serious Case Reviews[58] shows that 47 per cent of children were under one year of age but only 12 per cent were subject to a child protection plan.[59] Those who were not could have been receiving less intensive support, or may not have been identified as in need. In this context, the role of health visitors as a universal service seeing all children in their home environment with the potential to develop strong relationships with families is crucially important. A robust health visiting service delivered by highly trained skilled professionals who are alert to potentially vulnerable children can save lives.

5.22 Despite this, the number of health visitors has dropped by 10 per cent in the last three years[60] and case-loads are significantly higher than the recommended 300 families or 400 children,[61] with 40 per cent of health visitors handling case-loads of over 500 children and 20 per

58 Brandon, Marion, Pippa Belderson, Catherine Warren, David Howe, Ruth Gardner, Jane Dodsworth, Jane Black, *Analysing Child Deaths and Serious Injury though Abuse – What can we Learn? A Biennial Analysis of Serious Case Reviews 2003–05* (HM Government [DCSF], 2008)

59 Ofsted, *Analysing Child Deaths and Serious Injury through Abuse: What can we Learn? A Biennial Analysis of Serious Case Reviews 2003–2005*

60 Unite/Community Practitioners' and Health Visitors' Association Omnibus Survey, 2008

61 As recommended by the Community Practitioners' and Health Visitors' Association

cent over 1,000 children[62]. 69.2 per cent of health visitors say that they no longer have the resources to respond to the needs of the most vulnerable children.[63] Health visitors need time to properly support and assess children and to be competent and confident in doing so. There are very real risks to the welfare of children if this does not happen. The commitment to increase the number of health visitors in *Healthy lives, brighter futures*[64] is a helpful one but priority and resources need to be committed to achieving this aim.

5.23   Furthermore, there is confusion about the role of health visitors who provide a universal service and yet often are called upon to support families with complex needs. As the case-loads of social workers have risen there is also concern that health visitors are carrying child protection issues that once would have been referred on to children's social care services. This is both inappropriate and unmanageable for health visitors and needs to be addressed.

Recommendations

The Department of Health should prioritise its commitment to promote the recruitment and professional development of health visitors (made in *Healthy lives, brighter futures*) by publishing a national strategy to support and challenge Strategic Health Authorities to have a sufficient capacity of well trained health visitors in each area with a clear understanding of their role.

The Department of Health should review the Healthy Child Programme for 0–5-year-olds to ensure that the role of health visitors in safeguarding and child protection is prioritised and has sufficient clarity, and ensure that similar clarity is provided in the Healthy Child Programme for 5–19-year-olds.

5.24   The engagement of health professionals, particularly GPs in Children's Trusts, Local Safeguarding Children Boards, and other multi-agency forums for safeguarding children is very varied. A common concern raised during the production of this report is the difficulty in attracting 'designated' and 'named' health professionals, both in primary and secondary care, with responsibility for child protection. It appears that the safeguarding of vulnerable children is often not viewed as a priority for GPs in some areas. A range of measures has been

62 Unite/Community Practitioners' and Health Visitors' Association Omnibus Survey, 2008
63 Unite/Community Practitioners' and Health Visitors' Association Omnibus Survey, 2008
64 HM Government, *Healthy lives, brighter futures – the strategy for children and young people's health* (2009)

introduced to support GPs and child health professionals by the Department of Health, through the Care Services Improvement Partnership, and by many of the Royal Medical Colleges including the Royal College of General Practitioners (RCGP) and the Royal College for Paediatrics and Child Health. These support measures include a toolkit for GPs developed in partnership with the NSPCC, a secure website to enable 'named' and 'designated' professionals to share practice, the establishment of regional learning networks, and the piloting of an 'Influencing for Leadership' course. However, more needs to be done to ensure GPs are proactive in doing all they can to keep children safe. There needs to be suitable rigour in the child protection training for each GP which enables them to contribute effectively to a multi-agency approach to the well-being of children. This should include appropriate referral and information sharing training.

Recommendation

The Department of Health should promote the statutory duty of all GP providers to comply with child protection legislation and to ensure that all individual GPs have the necessary skills and training to carry out their duties. They should also take further steps to raise the profile and level of expertise for child protection within GP practices, for example by working with the Department for Children, Schools and Families to support joint training opportunities for GPs and children's social workers and through the new practice accreditation scheme being developed by the Royal College of General Practitioners.

5.25 Evidence to this report suggested that paediatricians are sometimes reluctant to become involved in child protection work. The Department of Health should take forward further work with paediatricians to understand and respond to their concerns and to enable them to become confident in carrying out their role.

> ### Recommendation
>
> The Department of Health should work with partners to develop a national training programme to improve the understanding and skills of the children's health workforce (including paediatricians, midwives, health visitors, GPs and school nurses) to further support them in dealing with safeguarding and child protection issues.

Police services

5.26 Concerns about the resourcing of child protection teams exist within a large number of police forces, particularly since other issues have taken on greater national significance.[65] Although not general, there is clearly an issue that, in a number of forces, child protection work is accorded low status and does not attract the most able and experienced police officers. Some forces that contributed to this report also described high vacancy rates within child protection teams and others have seen significant reductions in posts in the years since the initial response to Victoria Climbié.

5.27 Police services should take immediate action to review the staffing of child protection teams to ensure they are well resourced to ensure children's safety is not compromised. As with other professions, police officers must receive specialist training to work on child protection over and above core police training, including that of how best to talk and listen to children and young people often in distress.

> ### Recommendation
>
> The Home Office should take national action to ensure that police child protection teams are well resourced and have specialist training to support them in their important responsibilities.

65 Gardner, Ruth, and Marian Brandon, 'Child protection: crisis management or learning curve?' in *Public Policy Research* (December 2008 – February 2009)

IMPROVEMENT AND CHALLENGE

"There are only two lasting bequests we can hope to give our children. One is roots; the other, wings."

Hodding Carter[66]

6.1 There is a clear need for a determined focus on improvement of practice in child protection across all the agencies that support children. New ways should be created to share good practice and learn lessons when things go wrong. Within that context there is a need to strengthen the inspection processes of each of the services responsible for the safety of children. Inspection should not be a stand-alone activity. It should not be only an isolated snapshot. It must be accompanied by a robust developmental process aimed at achieving higher standards of service provision.

Inspection

6.2 Since April 2007, Ofsted have had responsibility for inspecting all local authority children's services, including safeguarding and child protection. This responsibility was previously held by the Commission for Social Care Inspection (CSCI). From 2005 to 2008, Ofsted (along with CSCI until 2006) undertook Annual Performance Assessments of local authorities' children's services which were largely paper-based and reported a performance rating for staying safe. Local authorities said in their evidence to this report that they were often dissatisfied with the rigour and quality of these assessments. In addition, Ofsted worked with the Healthcare Commission, Audit Commission and HMI Probation to undertake Joint Area Reviews (JARs) of children's services every three years. JARs looked at the performance of all local partners in safeguarding children. They involved a short on-site inspection fieldwork but the evidence to this report was critical about the depth and breadth of the fieldwork.

66 Hodding Carter (1907–72), US journalist and author

6.3   On 10 February 2009 Ofsted announced changes to the inspection of safeguarding from April 2009. In future they will undertake annual unannounced on-site inspections of the quality and effectiveness of arrangements for contact, referrals and assessment processes for safeguarding and child protection work. A full, announced, inspection will take place every three years (more often where services are inadequate) to evaluate the impact of the local authority, partners, and of the Local Safeguarding Children Board (LSCB) and Children's Trust in improving safeguarding outcomes. The three-yearly inspection programme will be carried out by inspectors from Ofsted and the new Care Quality Commission (that will take on the responsibilities of the Healthcare Commission on 1 April 2009). HMI Constabulary is considering its capacity to contribute to this programme. The inspections will include analysis of local audits of need and their role in driving services as well as on-site visits to scrutinise practice, case-loads, training and support for staff, management oversight, the impact of the LSCB and Children's Trust, and the views of children and young people and of stakeholders. These changes are very much needed and potentially pave the way for more effective challenge of safeguarding and, particularly, child protection services.

6.4   Due to the multi-agency nature of child safeguarding and protection it is vital that other inspectorates follow the lead of Ofsted in improving the rigour of their inspection of police and health services for safeguarding and child protection. Inspectorates should also demonstrate more joint working to prepare and follow up inspections ensuring that safeguarding services as a whole are understood and improved.

Recommendation

The Care Quality Commission, HMI Constabulary and HMI Probation should review the inspection frameworks of their frontline services to drive improvements in safeguarding and child protection in a similar way to the new Ofsted framework.

6.5   To be effective and respected in challenging the status quo, any inspection process needs to be able to demonstrate expert knowledge and understanding of the subject under consideration. In the past, weaknesses in some inspection processes have been as a result of lack of expertise and limited experience in child protection in the key inspection bodies, most notably within Ofsted. There is a shared view of those undergoing inspection that Ofsted's primary expertise lies in the education field and that, whilst some specialist child protection and social care inspectors transferred into Ofsted from the CSCI, many senior inspection managers and experienced inspectors were lost in the move. This needs to be addressed as a matter of urgency if the new inspection framework is to be effective.

> ### Recommendation
>
> Ofsted, the Care Quality Commission, HMI Constabulary and HMI Probation should take immediate action to ensure their staff have the appropriate skills, expertise and capacity to inspect the safeguarding and child protection elements of frontline services. Those Ofsted Inspectors responsible for inspecting child protection should have direct experience of child protection work.

Serious Case Reviews (SCRs)

6.6   SCRs are an important tool for learning lessons from the death of, or a serious incident involving, a child. They are now generally well established and have, in principle, support from all services. However, the purpose and processes of SCRs can be further developed to strengthen their impact on keeping children safe from harm.

The purpose of SCRs

6.7   *Working Together to Safeguard Children* set out the purpose of SCRs[67] both in identifying lessons about how professionals and agencies work together to safeguard and promote the welfare of children, and ensuring interagency working is improved as a result. Whilst reviewing lessons for interagency working is important, the evidence to this report has identified that weaknesses also exist within individual organisations from which lessons could be learned to protect children better from harm. To be effective, an SCR must include consideration of the lessons that can be learned within each of the services involved in a case, as well as how they cooperate together where there has been the death or serious harm of a child. This is not intended to change the purpose of SCRs as a learning exercise or to suggest they should become involved in blame or disciplinary proceedings. But the current remit of SCRs as set out in *Working Together to Safeguard Children* is too narrow and is at risk of not being sufficiently explicit

---

67 HM Government, *Working Together to Safeguard Children: A guide to interagency working to safeguard and promote the welfare of children* (2006), Paragraph 8.3

about the role of SCRs in learning lessons for individual organisations to allow a proper understanding of how children can be better protected from harm to be developed.

> ### Recommendation
>
> The Department for Children, Schools and Families should revise *Working Together to Safeguard Children* so that it is explicit that the formal purpose of Serious Case Reviews is to learn lessons for improving individual agencies, as well as for improving multi-agency working.

Conducting an SCR

6.8 Evidence submitted to this report indicates that the primary purpose of SCRs as a learning process to protect children more effectively in the future is in danger of being lost. This is a result both of confusion about the purpose of SCRs, which are sometimes perceived as holding individuals or agencies to account, and as a result of the SCR process itself, which does not currently lend itself to quick, effective reflection and the sharing of learning following a serious or tragic incident.

6.9 SCR panels have no powers to demand access to documents from agencies, and are entirely dependent upon the willing cooperation of all concerned. This presents a real difficulty for SCR panels in gathering all the information they need to understand a case properly and make recommendations on how similar tragedies can be avoided in future. The framework for SCRs needs to be reviewed to ensure that the SCR panel chairs have access to all of the relevant documents and staff they need to conduct a thorough and effective learning exercise.

> ### Recommendation
>
> The Department for Children, Schools and Families should revise the framework for Serious Case Reviews to ensure that the Serious Case Review panel chair has access to all of the relevant documents and staff they need to conduct a thorough and effective learning exercise.

6.10 Concerns have also been raised that the SCR process has become too focused on the writing of an often long and unwieldy report with insufficient focus by LSCBs on whether lessons are being learned from a child's death or serious injury and whether action plans are subsequently implemented. This needs to be addressed urgently to create a more streamlined learning process. Of the 45 SCRs which Ofsted assessed between April 2007 and March 2008 only 31per cent were completed within one year.[68] The guidance in *Working Together to Safeguard Children* that lessons should be implemented as soon as practicable needs strengthening to encourage LSCBs not to wait until an SCR is completed before doing so. To this end, there is good practice that can be adapted from the Metropolitan Police's Homicide Task Force and the National Patient Safety Agency's Root Cause Analysis Toolkit.[69]

Recommendation

The Department for Children, Schools and Families should revise *Working Together to Safeguard Children* to ensure Serious Case Reviews focus on the effective learning of lessons and implementation of recommendations and the timely introduction of changes to protect children.

Ofsted evaluation of SCRs

"Ofsted are evaluating SCRs as if they were an academic exercise. The real skill is in cascading the lessons to be learnt across all the multi-agency partners."   LSCB Board Member

6.11   Many of those who contributed to this report felt unsure about how Ofsted were making judgements on SCRs, or were concerned that too much emphasis was placed on the quality of the written report rather than on the SCR as an effective learning tool. Ofsted evaluation should focus on the quality of the process of the review, the adequacy of learning and change, professional practice, and the quality of recommendations in protecting children to ensure that they are actively driving improved outcomes and better safeguarding systems and this focus should be properly communicated to LSCBs.

---

68 Ofsted, *Learning lessons, taking action: Ofsted's evaluations of serious case reviews 1 April 2007 to 31 March 2008* (December 2008)

69 These single agency processes are still useful comparators in learning lessons quickly from serious incidents. The National Patient Safety Agency's Root Cause Analysis Toolkit can be found at www.npsa.nhs.uk/nrls/improvingpatientsafety/patient-safety-tools-and-guidance/rootcauseanalysis/

Recommendation

Ofsted should focus its evaluation of Serious Case Reviews on the depth of the learning a review has provided and the quality of recommendations it has made to protect children.

Case study F

Learning lessons from Serious Case Reviews

One local authority had experienced a number of child deaths and recognised the importance of learning lessons from each event, and of noticing trends over a number of SCRs.

The local authority has introduced a number of innovative methods to help practitioners and managers learn from previous cases. These have included the facilitation of workshops which have captured local and national issues and themes arising from SCRs, and the production of a highly effective CD recorded by six student social workers featuring the stories of children and young people who have died. The stories were taken from case material and told from the child's own perspective. They are a valuable though emotionally hard-hitting tool for further understanding the voices and views of the child, an issue important for all professionals involved in frontline services. Through these and other learning events, the local authority is able to evidence change and improvement through learning lessons and recognising recurring themes in their own SCRs. The learning is shared across agencies and is proving beneficial to social workers and health visitors especially.

The importance of confidentiality

6.12 SCRs inevitably include a great deal of case material that should remain confidential, not only to protect vulnerable people, but also because SCRs depend upon the cooperation of witnesses, often in a highly charged situation. Without this assurance many would be reluctant to participate in the process, rendering the task worthless. The future of SCRs depends, to a large degree, on the guarantee of confidentiality. Full reports should, therefore remain confidential beyond the immediate partners involved in a case, the relevant inspectorates, Government Offices and the relevant government departments.

Executive summaries of SCRs

6.13 The confidentiality of full SCRs makes the provision of a high-quality executive summary all the more important. Executive summaries should provide an accurate reflection of all the main points in the full report, include a copy of the full action plan, and provide the names of all the SCR panel members so that the public can have confidence that a senior and multi-agency panel, as well as an independent chair and independent author, have been in charge of the process.

Recommendation

The Department for Children, Schools and Families should revise *Working Together to Safeguard Children* to underline the importance of a high quality, publicly available executive summary which accurately represents the full report, contains the action plan in full, and includes the names of the Serious Case Review panel members.

When to conduct an SCR

6.14 There have been a number of calls for greater clarity in the guidance provided in *Working Together to Safeguard Children* on when an SCR should be conducted. DCSF data shows that there is considerable variation in the number of SCRs initiated in each region.[70] It is the conclusion of this report that further guidance on when to instigate an SCR would not be helpful due to the complexity and variety of cases for which an SCR may be conducted. However, Government Offices must continue to take a role in challenging SCR panels and LSCBs where they think inappropriate decisions have been made about conducting an SCR. Importantly, they should be certain that the cost and complexity of carrying out an SCR should not influence the decision of whether to conduct one. As SCRs are part of a learning process, the culture should be to encourage the undertaking of an SCR and no criticism should be made of an LSCB that chooses to carry out more SCRs. Such a review may also be used when a serious incident has been avoided to ensure lessons are learned about how to protect children better in future. There is a statutory requirement for every local area to have a child death overview panel which will consider every child death in the area, including those that may or may not be the result of an unavoidable accident or due to natural causes. The panel may decide to make a recommendation to the LSCB for an individual case to be looked at further by, for example, the LSCB commissioning an SCR. This may result in more SCRs being undertaken and further learning about when it is appropriate to commission an SCR.

Chairing of SCR panels

6.15 In carrying out an SCR it is important that the chairing and writing arrangements offer adequate scrutiny and challenge to all the agencies in a local area. For this reason, the chair of an SCR panel must be independent of all of those local agencies that were, or potentially could have been, involved in the case. A panel may be chaired by someone with similar responsibilities in another Children's Trust or may be fully independent of statutory services. However, they will need to be fully prepared for their role in conducting an effective scrutiny of each aspect of how the agencies responded to the needs of the child or young person. There should be training for SCR panel chairs available nationally and Government Offices must take the lead in ensuring there are enough people within a region who are trained and able to chair SCRs when the need arises. It is important that throughout the process, the SCR panel chair and all its members maintain the principle that the views of all partners are valid and equal so that appropriate challenge and robust dialogue can take place.

Independent authors

6.16 Similarly, a greater emphasis is needed on building a cohort of people skilled and able to write effective SCR reports. Many authorities have had difficulties in recruiting good quality authors and this has led to both delays and poor quality reports. SCR authors must be independent of those local agencies that were, or potentially could have been, involved in the case. An SCR author may or may not be the same person who chairs the SCR panel. The decision should be made according to the individual needs of the case in question. Training should be made available nationally for SCR authors and Government Offices should take the lead in ensuring they have enough high-quality trained authors in their region. It will remain the responsibility of the LSCB to take up references on those who have completed the training before appointing an independent author.

Recommendations

Local Safeguarding Children Boards should ensure all Serious Case Review panel chairs and Serious Case Review overview authors are independent of the Local Safeguarding Children Board and all services involved in the case and that arrangements for the Serious Case Review offer sufficient scrutiny and challenge.

All Serious Case Review panel chairs and authors must complete a training programme provided by the Department for Children, Schools and Families that supports them in their role in undertaking Serious Case Reviews that have a real impact on learning and improvement.

Government Offices must ensure that there are enough trained Serious Case Review panel chairs and authors available within their region.

Sharing SCRs with Inspectorates

6.17 To ensure that the learning from SCRs is driving safer systems and processes for children and young people, Ofsted, the Care Quality Commission, HMI Constabulary and HMI Probation (when appropriate) should have access to the full reports and should use them in the preparation for local inspections of children's services, health, police and probation where appropriate. This will ensure that the consequences of an inadequate SCR are felt by all partner agencies and not just the local authority. It should ensure also that inspectorates of the other agencies are able to assess whether the recommendations have been implemented.

Sharing learning from SCRs

6.18 Learning from SCRs needs to be shared quickly so that lessons are learned across different areas and agencies as quickly as possible. This should include the timely sharing of the executive summaries of SCR reports between local authorities, with the Association of Chief Police Officers, with Primary Care Trusts and with Strategic Health Authorities. In addition to this, Ofsted should produce more regular reports bringing together the lessons from SCR reports as well as drawing upon practice evaluated as part of their inspection function.

Recommendations

Ofsted should:

- share full Serious Case Review reports with HMI Constabulary, the Care Quality Commission, and HMI Probation (as appropriate) to enable all four inspectorates to assess the implementation of action plans when conducting frontline inspections;

- share Serious Case Review executive summaries with the Association of Chief Police Officers, Primary Care Trusts and Strategic Health Authorities to promote learning; and

- produce more regular reports, at six-monthly intervals, which summarise the lessons from Serious Case Reviews.

The role for a National Safeguarding Delivery Unit

6.19 In addition to the challenge that inspection systems provide and the learning that is shared when there is a tragic failure to protect a child from harm, there must be a continuing drive for improvement in the protection of children and young people that ensures the systems and practices become the best in the world at keeping children safe. It is clear that within the existing landscape every organisation has only a partial view. There is none that has the breadth of vision across frontline agencies responsible for keeping children safe from harm, or the authority to achieve improvements across all the services with responsibility for safeguarding and promoting the welfare of children.

6.20 Therefore a National Safeguarding Delivery Unit should be established that can work flexibly to take urgent action to challenge and support local services to improve provision for children and young people. The unit does not have to be a permanent presence in the landscape of safeguarding, but should be an authorative, agile organisation with an initial remit for three years, and sufficient programme resources, to create a real and early impact across children's services, health and police services, and in every Children's Trust across the country.

6.21 In order to have the authority to drive such changes the National Safeguarding Delivery Unit should report on progress every three months directly to the Cabinet Sub-Committee on Families, Children and Young People. In addition it should provide Parliament with an annual report on progress in improving the effectiveness and efficiency of child protection systems in this country.

6.22 The unit should be led by someone with the expertise, authority and ambition to drive change in safeguarding services. It should draw upon expertise from practising senior staff with frontline experience in safeguarding across children's services, police and health and other partners, and with experience of bringing about large-scale change in performance and culture. It should do this through secondments and project groups, ensuring that the most up-to-date expertise always informs its work.

Recommendation

The remit of the National Safeguarding Delivery Unit should include:

- working with the Cabinet Sub-Committee on Families, Children and Young People to set and publish challenging timescales for the implementation of recommendations in this report;

- challenging and supporting every Children's Trust in the country to implement recommendations within the agreed timescales, ensuring improvements are made in leadership, staffing, training, supervision and practice across all services;

- raising the profile of safeguarding and child protection across children's services, health and police;

- supporting the development of effective national priorities on safeguarding for all frontline services, and the development of local performance management to drive these priorities;

- leading a change in culture across frontline services that enables them to work more effectively to protect children;

- having regional representation with expertise on safeguarding and child protection that builds supportive advisory relationships with Children's Trusts to drive improved outcomes for children and young people;

- working with existing organisations to create a shared evidence base about effective practice including evidence-based programmes, early intervention and preventative services;

- supporting the implementation of the recommendations of Serious Case Reviews in partnership with Government Offices and Ofsted, and put in place systems to learn the lessons at local, regional and national level;

- gathering best practice on referral and assessment systems for children affected by domestic violence, adult mental health problems, and drugs and alcohol misuse, and provide advice to local authorities, health and police on implementing robust arrangements nationally; and

- commissioning training on child protection and safeguarding and on leading these services effectively for all senior political leaders and service managers across those frontline services responsible for safeguarding and child protection.

ORGANISATION AND FINANCE

"My first social worker was lovely, she was kind... I think she liked me"

Girl, 12[71]

Local Safeguarding Children Boards

7.1 Despite Local Safeguarding Children Boards (LSCBs) being relatively new, they are already having a positive impact on services for protecting children. Ofsted published 21 Joint Area Reviews of children's services between April to June 2008 and in 18 of those they reported that LSCBs are already making a significant positive difference to their local services. In many areas, LSCBs provide a vital role in building stronger partnership relationships, and in providing a central point of focus within local areas for safeguarding children. However, it is inevitable that, being newly developed, there is greater potential to drive improvements, particularly around an increase in their ability to challenge the standard of practice and in strategic leadership.

7.2 There is no single model for how an LSCB operates. The Department for Children, Schools and Families (DCSF) and the Department of Health have commissioned research from the Loughborough University into the structures and working arrangements of LSCBs.[72] Early results demonstrate that their scope, structures, membership, resourcing, and ways of working vary considerably from area to area with some models likely to be more effective than others. Despite the positive feedback about LSCBs from contributors to this report, it is evident that many LSCBs would welcome further advice on these issues to help them maximise their impact on outcomes for children. The interim findings of the research from Loughborough University will be published in spring 2009 and it will greatly assist in

71 Quotation taken from findings of research with children undertaken by 11 Million in January 2009 specifically for this report
72 Publication forthcoming

understanding the differences in practice emerging in LSCBs. This should be used to provide further guidance to local areas to assist them making the arrangements for their LSCB as effective as possible.

> ### Recommendation
>
> The Department for Children, Schools and Families must provide further guidance to Local Safeguarding Children Boards on how to operate as effectively as possible following the publication of the Loughborough University research on Local Safeguarding Children Boards later this year.

7.3   Whilst recognising the value of local flexibility, there must be a clear distinction between the roles and responsibilities between LSCBs and Children's Trusts to ensure appropriate challenge, scrutiny and impartiality. Where the Director for Children's Services (DCS) chairs the LSCB they must not also chair the Children's Trust. Where chairs are independent of the local authority they must be sufficiently experienced in statutory safeguarding and child protection services and should have access to training and support to enable them to carry out their role effectively. To support the role of the LSCB chair in challenging the work of the Children's Trust, it is important that the chair is selected with the agreement of a group of partners representing the key services involved in safeguarding and child protection locally and should not be removed without consultation with those partners.

> ### Recommendations
>
> The Children's Trust and the Local Safeguarding Children Board should not be chaired by the same person. The Local Safeguarding Children Board chair should be selected with the agreement of a group of multi-agency partners and should have access to training to support them in their role.
>
> Local Safeguarding Children Boards should include membership from the senior decision makers from all safeguarding partners, who should attend regularly and be fully involved as equal partners in Local Safeguarding Children Board decision making.

7.4 It is important that there is a strong relationship between the LSCB and the Children's Trust. Ultimately it is the Children's Trust that is responsible for improving the well-being of children in the area across all five *Every Child Matters* outcomes, including keeping children safe. The responsibilities of the LSCB, in ensuring that the multi-agency partners in each local area are co-operating to safeguard and promote the welfare of children effectively, are a fundamental part of the overarching responsibilities held by the Children's Trust. The LSCB should report to the Children's Trust on the effectiveness of safeguarding and promoting the welfare of children and should publish a report on improving outcomes for children on an annual basis. Their report, and regular dialogue between the Children's Trust and the LSCB, should demonstrate that all the functions of both the LSCB and the Children's Trust as set out in *Working Together* are being effectively discharged. This must include effective policies and procedures to keep children safe, including the policies and procedures for the safe recruitment of frontline staff, ensuring staff receive suitable training, and commissioning Serious Case Reviews when appropriate. The commitment by Ofsted to inspect the impact of LSCBs on outcomes for children from April 2009 is very welcome.

> ### Recommendation
>
> Local Safeguarding Children Boards should report to the Children's Trust Board and publish an annual report on the effectiveness of safeguarding in the local area. Local Safeguarding Children Boards should provide robust challenge to the work of the Children's Trust and its partners in order to ensure that the right systems and quality of services and practice are in place so that children are properly safeguarded.

Funding safeguarding and child protection

7.5 Local authority expenditure on children's social care has increased greatly in recent years, from £2.9 billion in 2000/01 to £5.5 billion in 2007/08.[73] This is combined with significant increases in funding for preventative help and support for children and young people in the form of children's centres, extended schools, targeted youth support and family and parenting support, which are indicative of the Government's commitment. However, there is a danger that these

73 NHS Information Centre, *Personal Social Services Expenditure and Unit Costs: England 2006/07* (available online at www.ic.nhs.uk/statistics-and-data-collections/social-care/adult-social-care-information/personal-social-services-expenditure-and-unit-costs:-england-2006-07)

worthwhile initiatives have drawn resources away from the challenges of child protection. Protecting children from harm demands skill, determination and, quite often, courage. It is a vitally important work that deserves our full support.

7.6 It is imperative that those making financial decisions on the safeguarding of children at national and local level accurately plan adequate provision around real need and risk factors, rather than historic spending or even numbers of children who are the subject of child protection plans. In doing so, they should ensure that sufficient resources are in place to support early intervention and preventative services in addition to ensuring child protection work is properly resourced. These two very critical functions of any children's services department should not be in competition for resources. The Children's Trust should also have responsibility in understanding how the budgets of other agencies support safeguarding and child protection, and the benefits of pooling resources to provide maximum effect.

7.7 There is particular pressure on safeguarding budgets as a result of funding arrangements for local authorities. Whilst 82 per cent of schools funding is provided through the Dedicated Schools Grant,[74] a ring-fenced grant, finance allocated for safeguarding children is not made through a specific protected grant. So there is no guarantee that funding provided by government for the purposes of keeping children safe from harm, and improving their well-being is used for these purposes. The lack of protection around budgets for safeguarding children has also left them at risk from the pressure upon councils to deliver efficiency savings under the 2004 Gershon Review of Public Sector Efficiency.[75] The Government should therefore take decisive action to protect budgets for safeguarding children, thereby ensuring consistent appropriate levels of investment across England in both early intervention and statutory child protection services.

74 Figure obtained from the Department for Children, Schools and Families
75 Gershon, Sir Peter, *Releasing resources for the frontline: Independent Review of Public Sector Efficiency* (HM Treasury, 2004)

Recommendations

The Department for Children, Schools and Families, the Department of Health, and the Home Office, together with HM Treasury, must ensure children's services, police and health services have protected budgets for the staffing and training for child protection services.

The Department for Children, Schools and Families must sufficiently resource children's services to ensure that early intervention and preventative services have capacity to respond to all children and families identified as vulnerable or 'in need'.

A national annual report should be published reviewing safeguarding and child protection spend against assessed needs of children across the partners in each Children's Trust.

LEGAL

> "Every child should be listened to, no matter how difficult they are to talk to."

Girl, 15[76]

Understanding the law

8.1   In this country there is a comprehensive legislative framework for protecting children and keeping them safe from harm. The Children Act 1989 reformed the law and was "the most comprehensive and far reaching reform of child law".[77] The Children Act 2004 introduced a statutory duty on local authorities and their partner agencies to cooperate to improve the well-being of children and embedded the five *Every Child Matters* outcomes in law. Further legislative change is not what is needed to protect children. However, it is vital that all professionals with responsibility for the welfare of children fully understand the legislative framework in relation to safeguarding and child protection, and have a clear understanding of their responsibilities in the process. This includes ensuring that legal advisers within a local authority receive high-quality initial training and continuing professional development in this area of law.

Who makes a care order?

8.2   It is for the local authority to decide whether they should take action to safeguard and promote the child's welfare such as applying for a care order. However, it is for the court to decide whether the threshold criteria are met and a care order should be made with respect to the child. As Baroness Hale of Richmond said in Re B (A Minor) (AP)

> *"It is to confuse the role of the local authority, in assessing and managing risk, in planning for the child, and deciding what action to initiate, with the role of the court in deciding where the truth lies and*

76 Quotation taken from findings of research with children undertaken by 11 Million in January 2009 specifically for this report.

77 Per Lord Mackay Children Bill (Hansard, H.L. Vol. 502, col. 488; 6 December 1988)

what the legal consequences should be. I do not under-estimate the difficulty of deciding where the truth lies but that is what the courts are for."

Pre-proceedings – the role of the local authority

8.3   New guidance for local authorities was issued in April 2008[78] that sets out the processes to be followed in making an application for a care or supervision order. It is essential that the local authority can put the evidence on which their decision to make the application is based before the court. This is the reason for the pre-proceedings checklist. Good preparation enables a case to proceed more quickly and to reach a permanent solution for the child. It is essential that the court is well-informed about the work that has taken place with families. The evidence should demonstrate that the parents understand the concerns that have been raised, the objectives and goals of any intervention, and the action taken by parents and the local authority and when such actions were reviewed.

8.4   However, whilst it is important that the correct documentation is in place for each case, the local authority should not delay making an application because of paperwork considerations if there is concern for a child that requires swift action in order to safeguard their welfare.

Public Law Outline

8.5   In April 2008 the Public Law Outline (PLO), a new approach to case management, was introduced to reduce delay in care proceedings. It is too soon to be clear about the impact of the introduction of the PLO, and in particular whether or not it has increased workloads and added to delays in the process. There is currently conflicting evidence, for instance, whilst a number of contributions to this report raised concerns about the impact of the PLO, in London, the number of care proceedings cases being completed in under 40 weeks in care centres has risen from 22 per cent to 36 per cent when comparing the data for the quarter before the introduction of the PLO with the latest data following its implementation.[79]

---

78 The Children Act 1989: Guidance and Regulations: Volume 1: Court Orders
79 From June 2007, the draft PLO was tested in ten 'initiative' areas selected by the President of the Family Division. In autumn 2007 the President sought feedback from Designated Family Judges in the initiative areas about how the draft PLO was operating. The information and experiences from these areas and a consultation (between June and September 2008) helped to inform the final version of the PLO

Court proceedings

8.6   A number of social workers and other professionals struggle with the adversarial nature of court proceedings. Appearing in court can be an intimidating experience for social workers and other professionals, and managing this alongside a continuing relationship with a family is challenging. It is therefore important that all staff are adequately trained before going to court. This should be part of both specialist child protection training and continuing professional development.

Court case delays

8.7   On average care proceedings take 45 weeks in the Family Proceedings courts and 56 weeks in County and High Courts.[80] It is clear that for many children the length of delay in a court case is unacceptable. Research shows there are a number of possible reasons for delays, including, for example, delays in completing reports, the need to balance the case-loads of children's guardians over time, the need to explore and test family placements, and delays in obtaining expert evidence.[81] The view of the Judiciary is that in the vast majority of cases the expertise of the professionals already involved with the child should be sufficient expertise and a national expert is rarely required to add weight to a case.

8.8   The Ministry of Justice needs to take immediate action to address the length of delays in care proceedings to ensure that it is delivering its commitment to meet the timetable for the child. The aim to have a case progression function in all courts will help ensure that courts are used most effectively. In addition to this, listing arrangements of hearings should be more effectively business managed to ensure that the time of all staff involved in family court proceedings is used most effectively. Particular thought should be given to the use of expert witnesses to ensure they are used only when appropriate and do not delay proceedings unnecessarily.

80 Family Court, County and High Courts 2008/09 provisional data, Ministry of Justice, England and Wales. Notes:
  (1)   Family Court data is from Family Case Tracker and FamilyMan. County Court and High Court data is from FamilyMan.
  (2)   Figures are for April to September 2008
  (3)   Care and supervision orders are included and are counted by child for Family Court figures and by order for County Court and High Court.
81 Masson, Judith, Julia Pearce and Kay Bader, *Care profiling study* (Ministry of Justice, March 2008): references the three studies as Booth, 1996; Lord Chancellor's Department, 2002; Finch, 2004

Court fees

8.9   Where a local authority intervenes in the interests of protecting a child, it is clearly inappropriate that court fees might be a factor in that decision. These matters must be handled with very great care and in the interests of the child. Placing a child in the care of the local authority is a serious step, and local authorities should be encouraged to bring cases to court where they believe a care order may be necessary to safeguard the child. A local authority's role in safeguarding children is of vital importance, and no barrier, however small, should stand in the way of local authorities exercising this function.

8.10   It is of concern that the need to pay a fee might sometimes present a barrier that could influence a local authority's decision as to whether or not to commence care proceedings, despite the fact that they are very small in comparison to the overall costs of obtaining a care order. It is likely that a large proportion of the reduction in care applications in spring 2008 was as a result of the introduction of the PLO, as local authorities familiarised themselves with the new guidelines. It is also clear that the Government did not take the decision to increase these court fees lightly and it was helpful, to an extent, that funding was transferred from the Ministry of Justice to local authorities in recognition of the increased fees. However, if, even in one case, a local authority is deterred in taking action, that is one case too many.

8.11   Given the level of concern expressed about this issue, it may well be that abolition of fees altogether in these cases would be the safest course. For this reason, the Ministry of Justice should undertake to hold an independent review of the impact of the fees in the coming months. Unless this review provides incontrovertible evidence that the fees were not acting as a deterrent, the fees should then be abolished for the financial year 2010/11 and the ensuing years, with the funding transferred from the local government settlement to the Ministry of Justice.

Recommendations

The Ministry of Justice should:

- lead on the establishment of a system-wide target that lays responsibility on all participants in the care proceedings system to reduce damaging delays in the time it takes to progress care cases where these delays are not in the interests of the child; and

- appoint an independent person to undertake a review of the impact of court fees in the coming months. In the absence of incontrovertible evidence that the fees had not acted as a deterrent, they should then be abolished from 2010/11 onwards.

COMPLETE LIST OF RECOMMENDATIONS

1.   The Home Secretary and the Secretaries of State for Children, Schools and Families, Health, and Justice must collaborate in the setting of explicit strategic priorities for the protection of children and young people and reflect these in the priorities of frontline services.

2.   A National Safeguarding Delivery Unit be established to report directly to the Cabinet Sub-Committee on Families, Children and Young People. It should have a remit that includes:

   - working with the Cabinet Sub-Committee on Families, Children and Young People to set and publish challenging timescales for the implementation of recommendations in this report;

   - challenging and supporting every Children's Trust in the country to implement recommendations within the agreed timescales, ensuring improvements are made in leadership, staffing, training, supervision and practice across all services;

   - raising the profile of safeguarding and child protection across children's services, health and police;

   - supporting the development of effective national priorities on safeguarding for all frontline services, and the development of local performance management to drive these priorities;

   - leading a change in culture across frontline services that enables them to work more effectively to protect children;

   - having regional representation with expertise on safeguarding and child protection that builds supportive advisory relationships with Children's Trusts to drive improved outcomes for children and young people;

   - working with existing organisations to create a shared evidence base about effective practice including evidence-based programmes, early intervention and preventative services;

- supporting the implementation of the recommendations of Serious Case Reviews in partnership with Government Offices and Ofsted, and put in place systems to learn the lessons at local, regional and national level;

- gathering best practice on referral and assessment systems for children affected by domestic violence, adult mental health problems, and drugs and alcohol misuse, and provide advice to local authorities, health and police on implementing robust arrangements nationally; and

- commissioning training on child protection and safeguarding and on leading these services effectively for all senior political leaders and service managers across those frontline services responsible for safeguarding and child protection.

Leadership and accountability

3. The Cabinet Sub-Committee on Families, Children and Young People should ensure that all government departments that impact on the safety of children take action to create a comprehensive approach to children through national strategies, the organisation of their central services, and the models they promote for the delivery of local services. This work should focus initially on changes to improve the child-focus of services delivered by the Department of Health, Ministry of Justice and Home Office.

4. The Government should introduce new statutory targets for safeguarding and child protection alongside the existing statutory attainment and early years targets as quickly as possible. The National Indicator Set should be revised with new national indicators for safeguarding and child protection developed for inclusion in Local Area Agreements for the next Comprehensive Spending Review.

5. The Department of Health must clarify and strengthen the responsibilities of Strategic Health Authorities for the performance management of Primary Care Trusts on safeguarding and child protection. Formalised and explicit performance indicators should be introduced for Primary Care Trusts.

6. Directors of Children's Services, Chief Executives of Primary Care Trusts, Police Area Commanders and other senior service managers must regularly review all points of referral where concerns about a child's safety are received to ensure they are sound in terms of the quality of risk assessments, decision making, onward referrals and multi-agency working.

7. All Directors of Children's Services who do not have direct experience or background in safeguarding and child protection must appoint a senior manager within their team with the necessary skills and experience.

8. The Department for Children, Schools and Families should organise regular training on safeguarding and child protection and on effective leadership for all senior political leaders and managers across frontline services.

9. Every Children's Trust should ensure that the needs assessment that informs their Children and Young People's Plan regularly reviews the needs of all children and young people in their area, paying particular attention to the general need of children and those in need of protection. The National Safeguarding Delivery Unit should support Children's Trusts with this work. Government Offices should specifically monitor and challenge Children's Trusts on the quality of this analysis.

Support for children

10. Ofsted should revise the inspection and improvement regime for schools giving greater prominence to how well schools are fulfilling their responsibilities for child protection.

11. The Department for Children, Schools and Families should revise *Working Together to Safeguard Children* to set out clear expectations at all points where concerns about a child's safety are received, ensuring intake/duty teams have sufficient training and expertise to take referrals and that staff have immediate, on-site support available from an experienced social worker. Local authorities should take appropriate action to implement these changes.

12. The Department of Health and the Department for Children, Schools and Families must strengthen current guidance and put in place the systems and training so that staff in Accident and Emergency departments are able to tell if a child has recently presented at any Accident and Emergency department and if a child is the subject of a Child Protection Plan. If there is any cause for concern, staff must act accordingly, contacting other professionals, conducting further medical examinations of the child as appropriate and necessary, and ensuring no child is discharged whilst concerns for their safety or well-being remain.

13. Children's Trusts must ensure that all assessments of need for children and their families include evidence from all the professionals involved

in their lives, take account of case histories and significant events (including previous assessments) and above all must include direct contact with the child.

14. Local authorities must ensure that 'Children in Need', as defined by Section 17 of the Children Act 1989, have early access to effective specialist services and support to meet their needs.

15. The Social Work Task Force should establish guidelines on guaranteed supervision time for social workers that may vary depending on experience.

16. The Department for Children, Schools and Families should revise *Working Together to Safeguard Children* to set out the elements of high quality supervision focused on case planning, constructive challenge and professional development.

17. The Department for Children, Schools and Families should undertake a feasibility study with a view to rolling out a single national Integrated Children's System better able to address the concerns identified in this report, or find alternative ways to assert stronger leadership over the local systems and their providers. This study should be completed within six months of this report.

18. Whether or not a national system is introduced, the Department for Children, Schools and Families should take steps to improve the utility of the Integrated Children's System, in consultation with social workers and their managers, to be effective in supporting them in their role and their contact with children and families, partners, services and courts, and to ensure appropriate transfer of essential information across organisational boundaries.

Interagency working

19. The Department for Children, Schools and Families must strengthen *Working Together to Safeguard Children*, and Children's Trusts must take appropriate action to ensure:

   - all referrals to children's services from other professionals lead to an initial assessment, including direct involvement with the child or young person and their family, and the direct engagement with, and feedback to, the referring professional;

- core group meetings, reviews and casework decisions include all the professionals involved with the child, particularly police, health, youth services and education colleagues. Records must be kept which must include the written views of those who cannot make such meetings; and

- formal procedures are in place for managing a conflict of opinions between professionals from different services over the safety of a child.

20. All police, probation, adult mental health and adult drug and alcohol services should have well understood referral processes which prioritise the protection and well-being of children. These should include automatic referral where domestic violence or drug or alcohol abuse may put a child at risk of abuse or neglect.

21. The National Safeguarding Delivery Unit should urgently develop guidance on referral and assessment systems for children affected by domestic violence, adult mental health problems, and drugs and alcohol misuse using current best practice. This should be shared with local authorities, health and police with an expectation that the assessment of risk and level of support given to such children will improve quickly and significantly in every Children's Trust.

22. The Department for Children, Schools and Families should establish statutory representation on Local Safeguarding Children Boards from schools, adult mental health and adult drug and alcohol services.

23. Every Children's Trust should assure themselves that partners consistently apply the Information Sharing Guidance published by the Department for Children, Schools and Families and Department for Communities and Local Government to protect children.

Children's workforce

24. The Social Work Task Force should:

- develop the basis for a national children's social worker supply strategy that will address recruitment and retention difficulties, to be implemented by the Department for Children, Schools and Families. This should have a particular emphasis on child protection social workers;

- work with the Children's Workforce Development Council and other partners to implement, on a national basis, clear progression routes for children's social workers;

- develop national guidelines setting out maximum case-loads of children in need and child protection cases, supported by a weighting mechanism to reflect the complexity of cases, that will help plan the workloads of children's social workers; and

- develop a strategy for remodelling children's social work which delivers shared ownership of cases, administrative support and multi-disciplinary support to be delivered nationally.

25.   Children's Trusts should ensure a named, and preferably co-located, representative from the police service, community paediatric specialist and health visitor are active partners within each children's social work department.

26.   The General Social Care Council, together with relevant government departments, should:

- work with higher education institutions and employers to raise the quality and consistency of social work degrees and strengthen their curriculums to provide high quality practical skills in children's social work;

- work with higher education institutions to reform the current degree programme towards a system which allows for specialism in children's social work, including statutory children's social work placements, after the first year; and

- put in place a comprehensive inspection regime to raise the quality and consistency of social work degrees across higher education institutions.

27.   The Department for Children, Schools and Families and the Department for Innovation, Universities and Skills should introduce a fully-funded, practice-focused children's social work postgraduate qualification for experienced children's social workers, with an expectation they will complete the programme as soon as is practicable.

28.   The Department for Children, Schools and Families, working with the Children's Workforce Development Council, General Social Care Council and partners should introduce a conversion qualification and English language test for internationally qualified children's social workers that ensures understanding of legislation, guidance and practice in England. Consideration should be given to the appropriate length of a compulsory induction period in a practice setting prior to formal registration as a social worker in England.

29.   Children's Trusts should ensure that all staff who work with children receive initial training and continuing professional development which enables them to understand normal child development and recognise potential signs of abuse or neglect.

30.   All Children's Trusts should have sufficient multi-agency training in place to create a shared language and understanding of local referral procedures, assessment, information sharing and decision making across early years, schools, youth services, health, police and other services who work to protect children. A named child protection lead in each setting should receive this training.

31.   The General Social Care Council should review the Code of Practice for Social Workers and the employers' code ensuring the needs of children are paramount in both and that the employers' code provides for clear lines of accountability, quality supervision and support, and time for reflective practice. The employers' code should then be made statutory for all employers of social workers.

32.   The Department of Health should prioritise its commitment to promote the recruitment and professional development of health visitors (made in *Healthy lives, brighter futures*) by publishing a national strategy to support and challenge Strategic Health Authorities to have a sufficient capacity of well trained health visitors in each area with a clear understanding of their role.

33.   The Department of Health should review the Healthy Child Programme for 0–5-year-olds to ensure that the role of health visitors in safeguarding and child protection is prioritised and has sufficient clarity, and ensure that similar clarity is provided in the Healthy Child Programme for 5–19-year-olds.

34.   The Department of Health should promote the statutory duty of all GP providers to comply with child protection legislation and to ensure that all individual GPs have the necessary skills and training to carry out their duties. They should also take further steps to raise the profile and level of expertise for child protection within GP practices, for example by working with the Department for Children, Schools and Families to support joint training opportunities for GPs and children's social workers and through the new practice accreditation scheme being developed by the Royal College of General Practitioners.

35.   The Department of Health should work with partners to develop a national training programme to improve the understanding and skills of the children's health workforce (including paediatricians, midwives,

health visitors, GPs and school nurses) to further support them in dealing with safeguarding and child protection issues.

36.   The Home Office should take national action to ensure that police child protection teams are well resourced and have specialist training to support them in their important responsibilities.

Improvement and challenge

37.   The Care Quality Commission, HMI Constabulary and HMI Probation should review the inspection frameworks of their frontline services to drive improvements in safeguarding and child protection in a similar way to the new Ofsted framework

38.   Ofsted, the Care Quality Commission, HMI Constabulary and HMI Probation should take immediate action to ensure their staff have the appropriate skills, expertise and capacity to inspect the safeguarding and child protection elements of frontline services. Those Ofsted Inspectors responsible for inspecting child protection should have direct experience of child protection work.

39.   The Department for Children, Schools and Families should revise *Working Together to Safeguard Children* so that it is explicit that the formal purpose of Serious Case Reviews is to learn lessons for improving individual agencies, as well as for improving multi-agency working.

40.   The Department for Children, Schools and Families should revise the framework for Serious Case Reviews to ensure that the Serious Case Review panel chair has access to all of the relevant documents and staff they need to conduct a thorough and effective learning exercise.

41.   The Department for Children, Schools and Families should revise *Working Together to Safeguard Children* to ensure Serious Case Reviews focus on the effective learning of lessons and implementation of recommendations and the timely introduction of changes to protect children.

42.   Ofsted should focus its evaluation of Serious Case Reviews on the depth of the learning a review has provided and the quality of recommendations it has made to protect children.

43.   The Department for Children, Schools and Families should revise *Working Together to Safeguard Children* to underline the importance of a high quality, publicly available executive summary which accurately represents the full report, contains the action plan in full, and includes the names of the Serious Case Review panel members.

44. Local Safeguarding Children Boards should ensure all Serious Case Review panel chairs and Serious Case Review overview authors are independent of the Local Safeguarding Children Board and all services involved in the case and that arrangements for the Serious Case Review offer sufficient scrutiny and challenge.

45. All Serious Case Review panel chairs and authors must complete a training programme provided by the Department for Children, Schools and Families that supports them in their role in undertaking Serious Case Reviews that have a real impact on learning and improvement.

46. Government Offices must ensure that there are enough trained Serious Case Review panel chairs and authors available within their region.

47. Ofsted should share full Serious Case Review reports with HMI Constabulary, the Care Quality Commission, and HMI Probation (as appropriate) to enable all four inspectorates to assess the implementation of action plans when conducting frontline inspections.

48. Ofsted should share Serious Case Review executive summaries with the Association of Chief Police Officers, Primary Care Trusts and Strategic Health Authorities to promote learning.

49. Ofsted should produce more regular reports, at six-monthly intervals, which summarise the lessons from Serious Case Reviews.

Organisation and finance

50. The Department for Children, Schools and Families must provide further guidance to Local Safeguarding Children Boards on how to operate as effectively as possible following the publication of the Loughborough University research on Local Safeguarding Children Boards later this year.

51. The Children's Trust and the Local Safeguarding Children Board should not be chaired by the same person. The Local Safeguarding Children Board chair should be selected with the agreement of a group of multi-agency partners and should have access to training to support them in their role.

52. Local Safeguarding Children Boards should include membership from the senior decision makers from all safeguarding partners, who should attend regularly and be fully involved as equal partners in Local Safeguarding Children Board decision making.

53.   Local Safeguarding Children Boards should report to the Children's Trust Board and publish an annual report on the effectiveness of safeguarding in the local area. Local Safeguarding Children Boards should provide robust challenge to the work of the Children's Trust and its partners in order to ensure that the right systems and quality of services and practice are in place so that children are properly safeguarded.

54.   The Department for Children, Schools and Families, the Department of Health, and the Home Office, together with HM Treasury, must ensure children's services, police and health services have protected budgets for the staffing and training for child protection services.

55.   The Department for Children, Schools and Families must sufficiently resource children's services to ensure that early intervention and preventative services have capacity to respond to all children and families identified as vulnerable or 'in need'.

56.   A national annual report should be published reviewing safeguarding and child protection spend against assessed needs of children across the partners in each Children's Trust.

Legal

57.   The Ministry of Justice should lead on the establishment of a system-wide target that lays responsibility on all participants in the care proceedings system to reduce damaging delays in the time it takes to progress care cases where these delays are not in the interests of the child.

58.   The Ministry of Justice should appoint an independent person to undertake a review of the impact of court fees in the coming months. In the absence of incontrovertible evidence that the fees had not acted as a deterrent, they should then be abolished from 2010/11 onwards.

LETTER TO LORD LAMING
FROM THE SECRETARY OF STATE FOR CHILDREN,
SCHOOLS AND FAMILIES

Rt Hon Ed Balls MP
Secretary of State

Sanctuary Buildings Great Smith Street Westminster London SW1P 3BT
tel: 0870 0012345 dcsf.ministers@dcsf.gsi.gov.uk

Lord Laming of Tewin
House of Lords
SW1A OPW

17 November 2008

Dear Lord Laming

PROGRESS REPORT ON SAFEGUARDING

The Children's Minister and I announced to Parliament on 12th November that we had asked you to prepare an urgent report of progress being made across the country to implement effective arrangements for safeguarding children. Thank you for agreeing to take this important work forward.

The reforms introduced by Government following the Victoria Climbié Inquiry set a very clear direction and have significantly strengthened the framework for safeguarding children. But it is vital we ensure that these reforms are being implemented systematically by all local agencies so that children in every part of the country receive the protection they need. Your work will be crucial in allowing us to assess progress being made, and to identify any barriers to effective, consistent implementation and how these might be overcome.

I would like your report to address three key questions:

1. What good practice has been successfully achieved in safeguarding children since the publication of the Victoria Climbié Inquiry Report? We would like you to set out the key features of this good practice, and whether it is being universally applied across the country, particularly in relation to:

    *   the effective implementation of safeguarding systems and procedures;
    *   inter-agency working;
    *   the development and deployment of professional workforce capacity; and
    *   effective systems of public accountability.

2. What are the key barriers, including in the legal process, that may impede efficient and effective work with children and families and that may be

department for
children, schools and families

preventing good safeguarding practice from becoming standard practice everywhere, for example in deciding whether an application should be made to take a child into care? Is the right balance being struck between the correct application of processes and the needs of the child?

3. What specific actions should be taken by Government and national and local agencies to overcome these barriers and accelerate systematic improvements in safeguarding practice across the country?

On 22nd October, I announced the terms of reference for the stocktake of Local Safeguarding Children Boards (LSCBs). One of the key issues being considered by this stocktake is the independence of LSCB chairs and whether the statutory guidance on this in *Working Together to Safeguard Children* needs to be revised. I also announced a study of Serious Case Reviews in order to identify what more can be done to improve the quality, consistency and impact of Serious Case Reviews as part of the overall system for safeguarding children and young people. I would like to bring both these pieces of work within the framework of your report.

It will of course be important that your report is informed by a wide range of views and experience and I know that you will be seeking views from key national and local stakeholders as you consider the issues. I will ensure you have all the professional support, and resource, you need to complete this task.

I look forward to receiving your report, with recommendations for action, early in the new year.

We are laying a copy of this letter in both libraries of the house.

Yours sincerely,

ED BALLS MP

GLOSSARY OF ABBREVIATIONS

ACPO	Association of Chief Police Officers
BBC	British Broadcasting Corporation
CAF	Common Assessment Framework
CAFCASS	Children and Family Court Advisory Support Service
CLG/DCLG	Communities and Local Government
CPD	Continuing Professional Development
CSCI	Commission for Social Care Inspection
CWDC	Children's Workforce Development Council
DA(FCY)	Domestic Affairs (Families, Children and Young People)
DCS	Director of Children's Services
DCSF	Department for Children, Schools and Families
GP	General Practitioner
GSCC	General Social Care Council
ICS	Integrated Children's System
JAR	Joint Area Review
LGA	Local Government Association
LSCB	Local Safeguarding Children Board
MP	Member of Parliament
NHS	National Health Service
NQSW	Newly Qualified Social Worker
NSPCC	National Society for the Prevention of Cruelty to Children
PCT	Primary Care Trust
PLO	Public Law Outline
RCGP	Royal College of General Practitioners

SCIE	Social Care Institute for Excellence
SCR	Serious Case Review
SHA	Strategic Health Authority
SOLACE	Society of Local Authority Chief Executives and Senior Managers
SWTF	Social Work Task Force
UN	United Nations

LIST OF LORD LAMING'S SECRETARIAT AND ADVISERS

Secretariat to the Lord Laming Report

Jenny Lawrence
Sharon McHale
Anne Mason
Benjamin Nicholls
Katharine O'Brien
Victoria Saunders

Advisers to the Report

Ann Baxter *Director of Children's Services, London Borough of Camden*
Jacky Tiotto *Senior National Adviser, Improvement and Development Agency (IDeA)*

Lord Laming is also grateful for contributions from

Dan Cooke, Anne Gair, Roger Parr, Sarah Wolstenholme

Printed in the UK for The Stationery Office Limited
on behalf of the Controller of Her Majesty's Stationery Office
ID 6079455 03/09
Printed on Paper containing 75% recycled fibre content minimum.